BHAGAT SINGH
Jail Diary

BHAGAT SINGH
Jail Diary

The Original Copy of Jail Diary of Shaheed-E-Azam Bhagat Singh

---

"They may kill me, but they can not kill my ideas"

Presented by

Yadvinder Singh Sandhu

(Grandson of Shaheed Bhagat Singh)

PRABHAT PRAKASHAN

ISO 9001: 2008 Publishers

Published by
PRABHAT PRAKASHAN
4/19 Asaf Ali Road,
New Delhi-110 002 (INDIA)
Tele : +91-11-23289777
e-mail: prabhatbooks@gmail.com

ISBN 978-93-5266-733-8
BHAGAT SINGH Jail Diary
Presented by Yadvinder Singh Sandhu

Edition
23 March, 2018

Price
₹ 800.00 (Rupees Eight Hundred only)

Printed at
R-Tech Offset Printers, Delhi

Late Shri Babar Singh Sandhu

(Nephew, Shaheed Bhagat Singh and S/o Shri Kulbir Singh)

"In the beloved memory of my loving father Shri Babar Singh Sandhu, It was the dream of my father to bring out the sacrifice of Shaheed Bhagat Singh through the 'Jail Diary' of martyr". I wish that his sacrifice will be relived again in the heart of the people.

PREFACE

Whenever we read of Bhagat Singh, a question always comes up — from where did he get inspiration, courage and power to do all that he did at such a young age — he was yet to be 24 when he was hanged? The present work can help us to a large extent in finding an answer to this question.

This book is an assimilation of thoughts, of great philosophers, thinkers, writers and leaders, such as freedom, justice, dignity and honour drawn from various different senses by Bhagat Singh during his last imprisonment (1929-1931) in the Central Jail, Lahore (Punjab). Bhagat Singh wrote these pages for Indians to tell them what is freedom, what is liberty and how to snatch these noble things from the soulless and ruthless Britishers who had reduced Indians into debased and downtrodden citizens.

These '*Jail Diary*' are written in a beautiful cloth-bound (red) notebook. It consists of 202 leaves (404 pages) of a little over 21 cm x 16 cm size, tied together with a long tag. Each page is stamped in black with its number at the upper right hand corner. In order to avoid any adverse effect of weather, dust, etc., the pages have been laminated. This has, unfortunately, affected the quality of our scanning. The following entry on page 1 of the 'notebook' shows that it was handed over to Bhagat Singh by the jail authorities on 12th September, 1929.

The Jail Diary was handed over, along with other belongings of Bhagat Singh, to his father, Sardar Kishan Singh after Bhagat Singh's execution. After Sardar Kishan Singh's death, the notebook (along with other papers of Bhagat Singh) was passed on to his son, Shri Kubir Singh. After his death, it has passed to his son, Shri Babar Singh. It was the dream of Shri Babar Singh that the

Indian masses also get to know through this jail diary what were the actual thoughts of Bhagat Singh and general people can also see the original writings of Bhagat Singh because he is the hero of every caste, religion, poor, rich, farmers, labourers.

Bhagat Singh's deep thinking and vision, love for mankind can be seen by his these words, "Our political parties consist of men who have but one idea, i.e. to fight against the alien rulers. That idea is quite laudable, but cannot be termed a revolutionary idea. We must make it clear that revolution does not merely mean an upheaval or a sanguinary strife. Revolution necessarily implies the programme of systematic reconstruction of society on new and better adapted basis, after complete destruction of the existing state of affairs (i.e. regime)."

Page 43 of his jail diary shows his thoughts on man and mankind: "I am a man and all that affects mankind concerns me."

Bhagat Singh was a full-blooded revolutionary and a clear sighted visionary; he looked to the future. In fact, future was in his bones.

What was, one might ask, that future like which Bhagat Singh had envisioned? How did he want to translate it into reality? In the present circumstances, Bhagat Singh's Jail *Diary* alone can answer these questions.

This book would not be complete without the blessings of Sh. Jitender Mehraji (Babaji), President Akhil Bharatiya Khatri Sabha, my mother Smt. Surinder Kaur, my sister Mrs Manjula Toor, my brother-in-law Mr Bhupender Singh Toor.

I am very much thankful to advocate Tarishi Mahajan for giving me the motivation, inspiration and support to make this book happen in real.

I am thankful to the following people for their continuous support—S.K. Sharma, Umed Singh, Sharif Choudhary, Vipin Jha, Deepak Sharma (Senior Journalist), Om Prakash (Senior Correspondent) & Ms. Anita Bhati (Senior Correspondent).

—Yadvinder Singh Sandhu

AIM OF LIFE

"The aim of life is no more to control mind, but to develop it harmoniously; not to achieve salvation hereafter, but to make the best use of it here below, and not to realise truth, beauty and good only in contemplation, but also in the actual experience of daily life; social progress depends not upon the ennoblement of the few but on the enrichment of the many; and spiritual democracy or universal brotherhood can be achieved only when there is an equality of opportunity in the social, political and industrial life."

(Bhagat Singh)

Sardar Arjun Singh
(Grandfather of Shaheed Bhagat Singh)

Sardar Kishan Singh
(Father of Shaheed Bhagat Singh)

Sardar Sawarn Singh
(Uncle of Shaheed Bhagat Singh)

Sardar Ajit Singh
(Uncle of Shaheed Bhagat Singh)

Smt. Vidyavati
(Mother of Shaheed Bhagat Singh, also known as Punjab Mata)

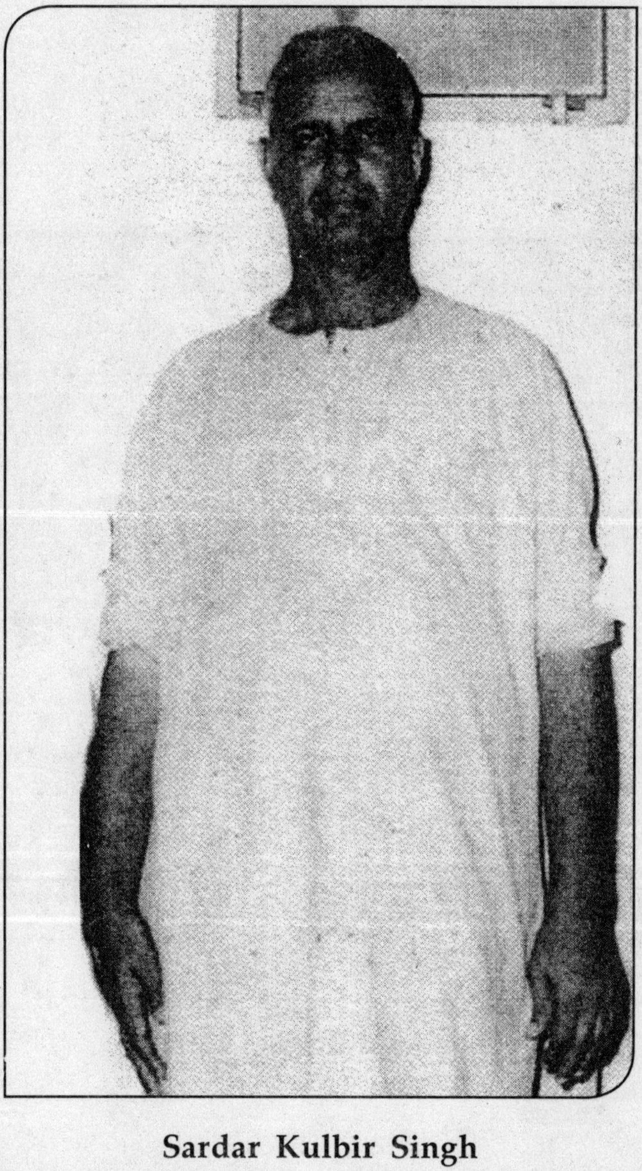

Sardar Kulbir Singh
(Real younger brother of Shaheed Bhagat Singh)

Brother Sardar Kulbir Singh and Smt. Vidyavati mother of Shaheed Bhagat Singh

Shaheed Bhagat Singh
(As a Child)

Shaheed Bhagat Singh
(As a Teenager)

Shaheed Bhagat Singh

Shaheed Bhagat Singh
(In jail, after his first arrest)

Shaheed Bhagat Singh

Shaheed Bhagat Singh
(A group photo of his college days, Bhagat Singh encircled)

Late Shri Babar Singh during childhood
(Nephew of Shaheed Bhagat Singh)
along with his grandmother Smt. Vidyavati

Late Babar Singh paying tribute to
Shaheed Bhagat Singh

Sardar Ajit Singh with Lokmanya Tilak and Aurobindo Ghosh
at Surat Congress in 1907

Sardar Ajit Singh with Sardar Kulbir Singh

Shri Puran Chand Azad welcoming Sardar Ajit Singh at Lahore on behalf of Congress Committee

Sardar Kulbir Singh sitting along with his father Sardar Kishan Singh

Shaheed Chandrasekhar Azad

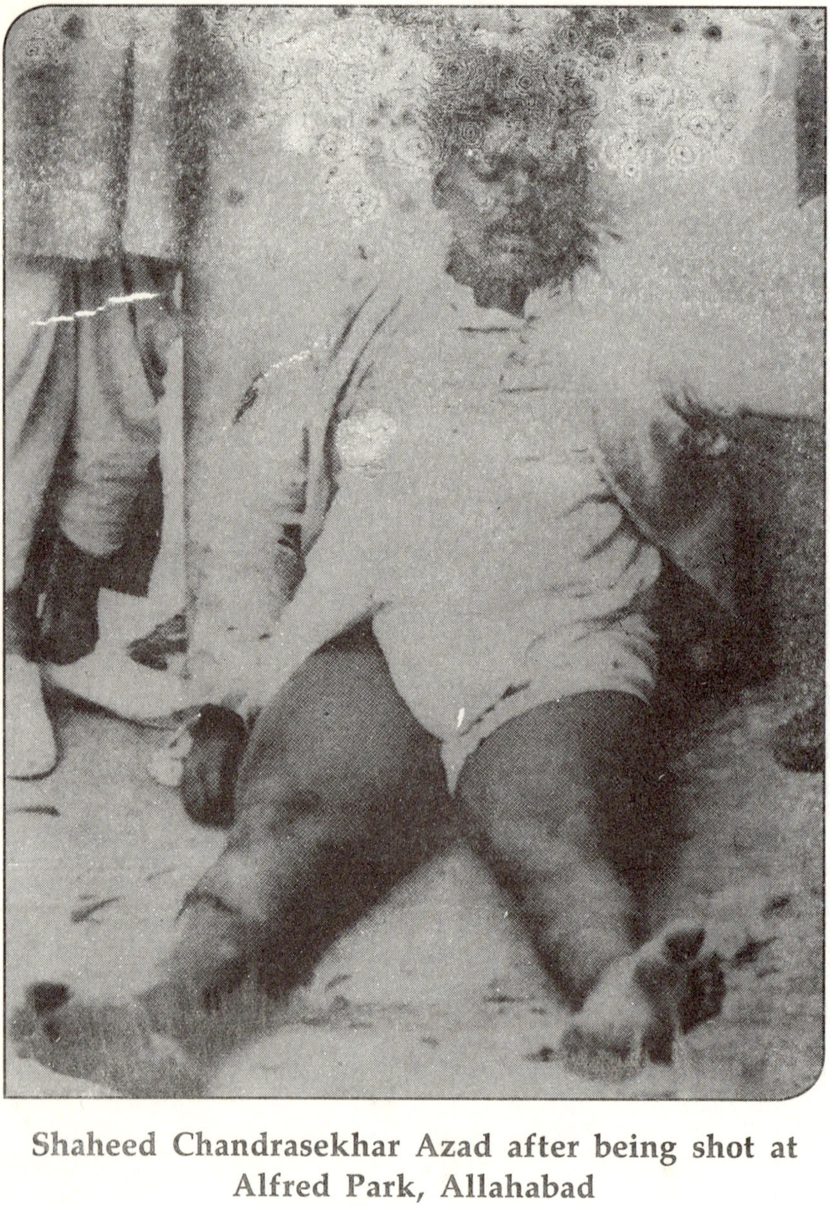

Shaheed Chandrasekhar Azad after being shot at Alfred Park, Allahabad

Postal stamp issued by Government of India on
Shaheed Bhagat Singh

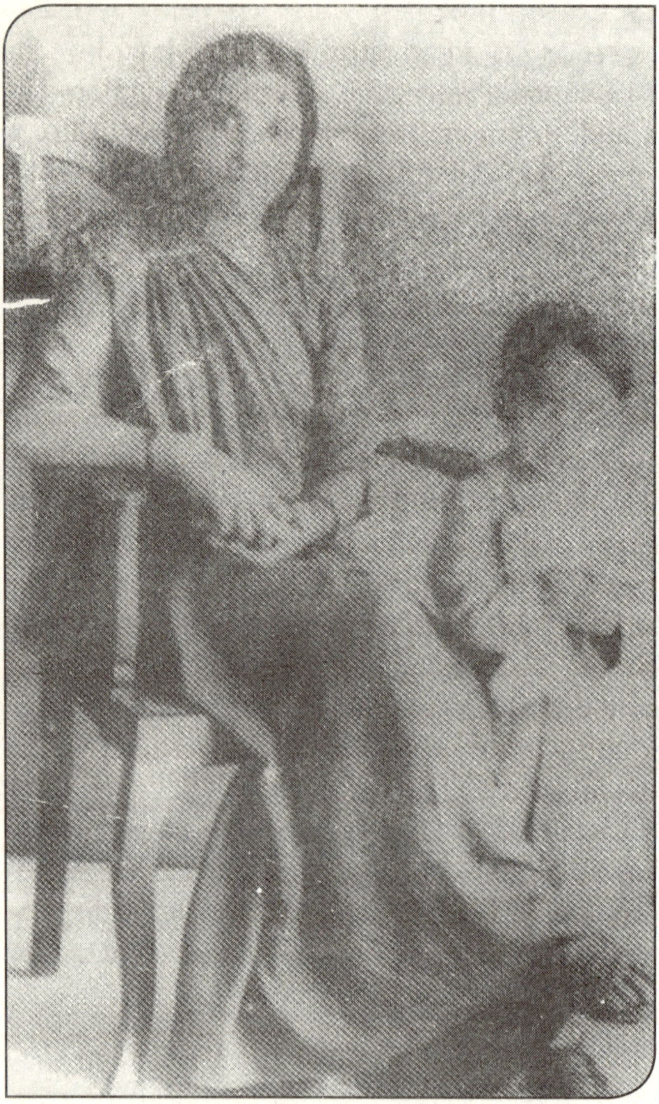

Durga Bhabhi with her son Sachin. She helped Bhagat Singh in escaping from Lahore

The Tribune

LAHORE, WEDNESDAY, APRIL 10, 1929 — Price:—One Anna

BOMB EXPLOSION IN LEGISLATIVE ASSEMBLY.

Finance Member Injured.

MEMBERS RUSH OUT IN PANIC.

President Patel Adjourns the House.

BOMBS THROWN

TWO young men, one a Panjabi and the other a Bengali entered the Legislative Assembly, dropped Red leaflets, threw bombs and fired pistols. They were arrested.

MEMBERS INJURED

Report of throwing of the bomb in the Assembly.

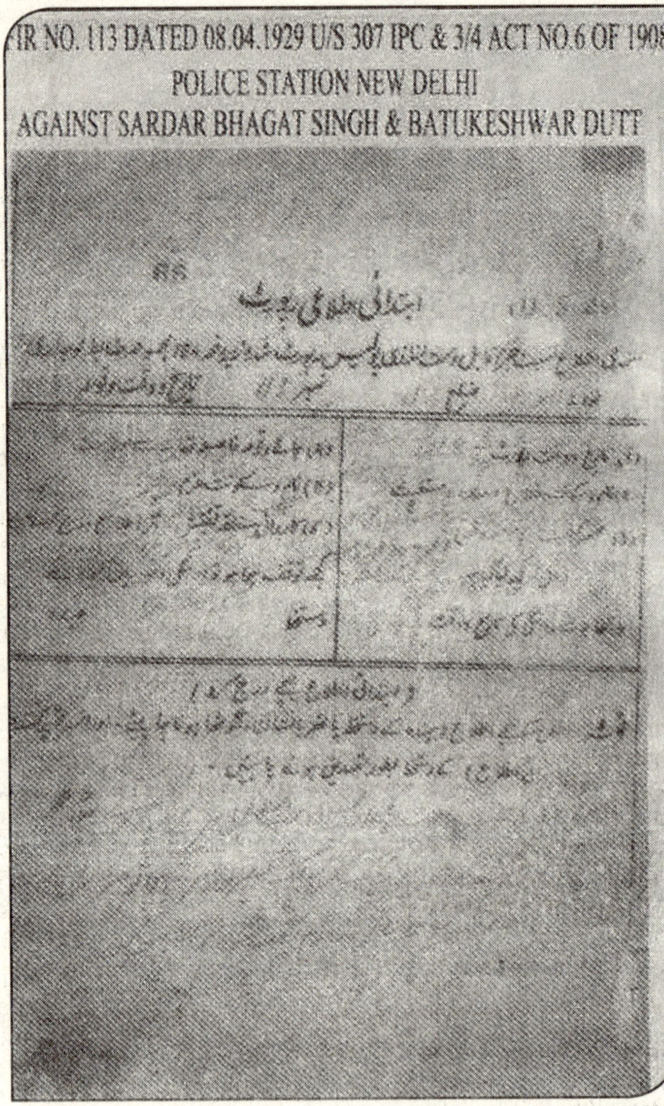

FIR NO. 113 DATED 08.04.1929 U/S 307 IPC & 3/4 ACT NO.6 OF 1908
POLICE STATION NEW DELHI
AGAINST SARDAR BHAGAT SINGH & BATUKESHWAR DUTT

Courtesy : Police Museum, Delhi

Copy of the FIR of the so-called 'Bomb outrage'

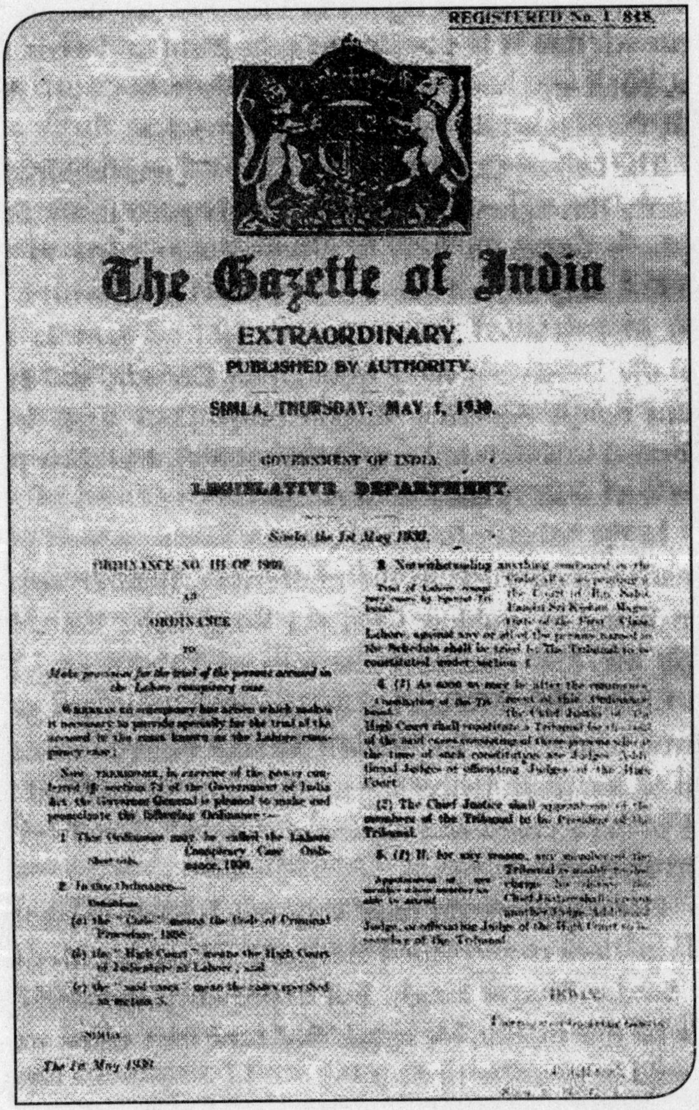

REGISTERED No. L. 848.

The Gazette of India

EXTRAORDINARY.

PUBLISHED BY AUTHORITY.

SIMLA, THURSDAY, MAY 1, 1930.

GOVERNMENT OF INDIA.

LEGISLATIVE DEPARTMENT.

Simla, the 1st May 1930.

ORDINANCE NO. III OF 1930.

AN

ORDINANCE

TO

Make provision for the trial of the persons accused in the Lahore conspiracy case.

WHEREAS an emergency has arisen which makes it necessary to provide specially for the trial of the accused in the cases known as the Lahore conspiracy case;

NOW, THEREFORE, in exercise of the power conferred by section 72 of the Government of India Act, the Governor General is pleased to make and promulgate the following Ordinance:—

1. This Ordinance may be called the Lahore Conspiracy Case Ordinance, 1930. *Short title.*

2. In this Ordinance,— *Definitions.*

(a) the "Code" means the Code of Criminal Procedure, 1898;

(b) the "High Court" means the High Court of Judicature at Lahore; and

(c) the "said cases" means the cases specified in section 3.

3. Notwithstanding anything contained in the Code, all [illegible] pending in the Court of Rai Sahib Pandit Sri Kishan, Magistrate of the First Class, Lahore, against any or all of the persons named in the Schedule shall be tried by the Tribunal to be constituted under section 4. *Trial of Lahore conspiracy cases by Special Tribunal.*

4. (1) As soon as may be after the commencement of this Ordinance the Chief Justice of the High Court shall constitute a Tribunal for the trial of the said cases consisting of three persons who at the time of such constitution are Judges, Additional Judges or officiating Judges of the High Court. *Constitution of the Tribunal.*

(2) The Chief Justice shall appoint one of the members of the Tribunal to be President of the Tribunal.

5. (1) If, for any reason, any member of the Tribunal is unable to discharge his duties, the Chief Justice shall appoint another Judge, Additional Judge, or officiating Judge of the High Court to be member of the Tribunal. *Appointment of new member when member unable to attend.*

[illegible]

The 1st May 1930.

[illegible]

The Tribunal's gazetted notification, May 1930

The Tribune.

VOL. LI. NO. 70 LAHORE, WEDNESDAY, MARCH 25, 1931. Price One Anna

BHAGAT SINGH, RAJGURU AND SUKHDEV EXECUTED.

NO "LAST INTERVIEW" WITH RELATIONS.

Shouts Emerge From Jail.

DEAD BODIES SECRETLY DISPOSED OF

Removed to Distant Place.

Thick Veil of Secrecy.

Relations' Futile Quest for Dead Bodies.

Bhagat Singh's Letter

Congress Leaders' Feeling.

Optical Instruments

After the hanging of Shaheed Bhagat Singh, next day the published copy of English Newspaper 'Tribune'

Sardar Ajit Singh at Lahore on his arrival after exile of 38 years. Those receiving him included Yash and Kulbir Singh, Mata Harnam Kaur, Sardar Kishen Singh

FILE
NOTE BOOK

BHARATI BHAVAN
BOOKSELLERS & PUBLISHERS
LAHORE

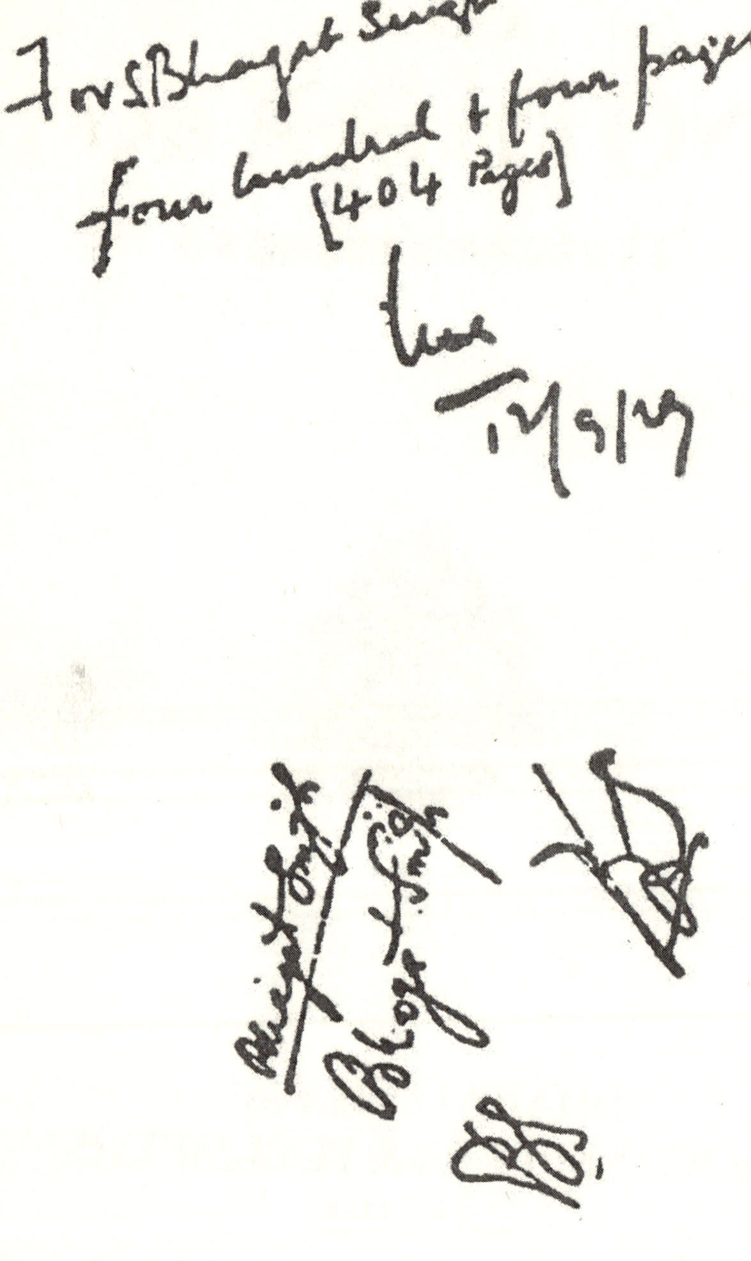
For S. Bhagat Singh
four hundred + four pages
[404 Pages]

Jail Diary-1

For Bhagat Singh
Four Hundred & four pages
[404 pages]

Signed/(Illegible)
(Jail authority, Lahore)
12.9.(19)29

Signed/(Bhagat Singh)
Signed/(Bhagat Singh)
Short initials/(BS)
Short initials/(BS)

* Page 2 is blank

Signed [illegible]

[Jail Authority]
12.9.29

* Page 4 is blank

Land measurements:-

German 20 hectares = 50 acres. i.e. 1 hectare = $2\frac{1}{2}$ acre

LAND MEASUREMENTS

German 20 hectares: 50 acres, i.e., 1 hectare = 2½ acres

0

Freedom from Poverty

The "freedom of property" . . . as far as the small capitalists and peasant-proprietors are concerned, became "freedom from property."

Marriage itself remained, as before, the legally recognized form, the official cloak of prostitution . . .

[Socialism: Scientific and Utopian]

— : o : —

Eternal Bondage

"An eternal being created human society as it is today and submission to 'superiors' and 'authority' is imposed on the 'lower' classes by divine will." This suggestion, coming from pulpit, platform and press, has hypnotised the minds of men and proves to be one of the strongest pillars of exploitation.*

{Translator's Preface to Origin of the Family}

FREEDOM FROM POVERTY

The 'freedom of property'... as far as the small capitalists and present proprietors are concerned, became 'freedom from poverty.'
Marriage itself remained, as before, the legally recognised form, the official cloak of prostitution...

[Sism Scientific and Utopian]

———— : * : ————

MENTAL BONDAGE

"An eternal being created human society as it is today, and submission to 'superiors' and 'authority' is imposed on the 'lower' classes by divine will." This suggestion, coming from pulpit, platform and press, has hypnotised the minds of men and proves to be one of the strongest pillars of exploitation.

{Translator's Preface to
Origin of the Family}

The Origin of the Family
by Engels.

Morgan was the first to make an attempt at introducing a logical order into the history of primeval society.

He divides it into three main epochs:—

1. Savagery 2. Barbarism. 3. Civilization

1. Savagery re-divided into three stages.

1. Lower 2. middle 3. Higher.

1. Lower Stage of Savagery:—

Infancy of human race. (1) Living in trees. (2) Fruits, nuts and roots serving as food. (3) The formation of articulated speech is the principal result of that period.

2. Middle Stage:—

Venison = Animal flesh taken in hunting

1. Fire discovered. 2. Fish being used. food. (3) Hunting stone implements invented. (4) cannibalism comes into existence.

3. Higher Stage:—

1. Bow and arrow. No pottery. 2. Village settlements. (3) Timber used for building (4) Cloth weaver.

Bow and arrows were for the stage of savagery what the sword was for barbarism and the fire arm for civilization the weapon of supremacy.

Jail Diary-7

THE ORIGIN OF THE FAMILY

By Engels

Morgan was the first to make an attempt at introducing a logical order into the history of primeval society.

He divides it into three main epochs:

1. Savagery 2. Barbarism 3. Civilisation

1. Savagery re-divided into three stages:

1. Lower 2. Middle 3. Higher

1. Lower Stage of Savagery:

Infancy of human race. Living in trees. (2) Fruits, nuts and roots serving as food. (3) The formation of articulated speech is the principal result of that period.

2. Middle Stage:

Vension animal flesh taken by hunting { 1. Fire discovered. 2. Fish being used as food. 3. For hunting stone implements invented. 4. Caninbalism comes into existence.

3. Higher Stage:

1. Bow and arrow. No pottery. 2. Village settlements.

3. Timber used for building. 4. Cloth weaved.

Bows and arrows were for the stage of savagery what the sword was for barbarism and the firearm for civilisation, the weapon of supremacy.

2. Barbarism:—

1. Lower Stage:—

1. Introduction of pottery. At first wooden pots were covered with layers of earth, but afterwards earthen pots were discovered.
2. Human races divided into two distinct classes. (1) Eastern who tamed animals and ~~grew~~ had grain. (2) Western who had only 'corn'

2. Middle Stage:—

1. (a) Western hemisphere i.e. in America they grew food plants, cultivation and irrigation, and baked bricks for house-building.
(b) Eastern:— They domesticated animals, for milk and flesh. No cultivation in this stage yet.

3. Higher Stage:—

(1) melting of iron ore
(2) Invention of letter script and its utilization for writing records.
This stage is richer in inventions. This is the period of Greek heroes.
(3) Iron ploughshare drawn by animals to grow corn on a larger scale.
(4) Clearing of forests, and iron axe and iron spade used.
(5) Great attainments:— (1) Improved iron tools, (2) the bellows (3) hand mill (4) Potter's wheel, (5) Preparation of oil and wine (6) fashioning metals (7) wagon and chariot (8) Ship building.

2. Barbarism

1. Lower Stage:

   1. Introduction of pottery. At first, wooden pots were covered with layers of earth, but afterwards earthen pots were discovered.

   2. Human races were divided into two distinct classes:

      (1) Eastern were those who tamed animals and had grain.

      (2) Western were those who had only corn.

2. Middle Stage:

   1. (a) Western hemisphere, i.e. in America, they grew food plants (cultivation and irrigation), and baked bricks for house-building.

      (b) Eastern: They domesticated animals for milk and flesh. No cultivation in this stage yet.

3. Higher Stage:

   (1) Melting of iron ore.

   (2) Invention of letter script and its utilisation for writing records. This stage is richer in inventions. This is the period of Greek heroes.

   (3) Iron ploughs are drawn by animals to grow corn on a large scale.

   (4) Clearing of forests, and iron axe and iron spade used.

   (5) Great attainments: (1) Improved iron tools, (2) The bellows, (3) Handmill, (4) Potter's wheel, (5) Preparation of oil and wine, (6) Fashioning metals, (7) Wagon and chariot, (8) Ship-building.

9. Artistic Architecture, 10, Towns and forts built.
11. Homeric Epochs and entire mythology.

With these attainments Greeks enter the third stage the 'Civilization'.

To sum up :-

1. Savagery — time of predominating appropriation of finished natural products; human ingenuity invents mainly tools useful in assisting this appropriation.

2. Barbarism :— time of acquiring knowledge of cattle raising, of agriculture and of new method for increasing the productivity of nature by human agency.

3. Civilization :— Time of learning a wider utilization of natural products, of manufacturing and of art.

"We have, then, three main forms of the family corresponding in general to the three main stages of human development.

1. For savagery," group marriage
2. For barbarism the pairing family
3. For civilization, monogamy supplemented by adultery and prostitution. Between the pairing family and monogamy, in the higher stage of barbarism, the rule of men over female slaves and polygamy is inserted.

pp. 90

(9) Artistic architecture, (10) Towns and forts built, (11) Homeric epochs and entire mythology.

With these attainments, Greeks entered the third stage — the 'civilisation'! To sum up:

1. Savagery: Time of predominating appropriation of finished natural products; human ingenuity invents mainly tools useful in assisting this appropriation.
2. Barbarism: Time of acquiring knowledge of cattle raising, of agriculture and of new methods for increasing the productivity of nature by human agency.
3. Civilisation: Time of learning a wider utilisation of natural products, of manufacturing and of art.

———————— : * : ————————

We have, then, three main forms of the family corresponding in general to the three main stages of human development:

1. for savagery, group marriage
2. for barbarism, the pairing family
3. for civilisation, monogamy supplemented by adultery and prostitution. Between the pairing family and monogamy, in the higher stage of barbarism, the rule of men over female slaves and polygamy is inserted.

~~But it says~~

Defects of marriage

Especially a long engagement is in nine cases out of ten a perfect training school of adultery. PP. 91

Socialist Revolution and marriage Institution!

We are now approaching a social revolution, in which the old economic foundations of monogamy will disappear just as surely as those of its complement, prostitution. Monogamy arose through the concentration of considerable wealth in one hand, a man's hand — and from the endeavour to bequeath this wealth to the children of this man to the exclusion of all others. This necessitated monogamy on the woman's, but not on the man's part. Hence this monogamy of women in no way hindered open or secret polygamy of men.

Now the impending social revolution will reduce this whole care of inheritance to a minimum by changing at least the overwhelming part of permanent and inheritable wealth — the means of production — into social property. Since monogamy was caused by economic conditions, will it appear when these causes are abolished?

PP. 91

DEFECTS OF MARRIAGE

Especially a long engagement is in nine cases out of ten, a perfect training school of adultery.

SOCIALISTIC REVOLUTION AND MARRIAGE INSTITUTION

We are now approaching a social revolution, in which the old economic foundations of monogamy will disappear just as surely as those of its complement, prostitution. Monogamy arose through the concentration of considerable wealth in one hand — a man's hand — and from the endeavour to bequeath this wealth to the children of this man to the exclusion of all others. This necessitated monogamy on the woman's part but not on the man's part. Hence, this monogamy of women in no way hindered open or secret polygamy of women.

Now the impending social revolution will reduce this whole case of the inheritance to a minimum by changing at least the overwhelming part of permanent and inheritable wealth — the means of production — into social property. Since monogamy was caused by economic conditions, will it disappear when these causes are abolished?

"Ah, my Beloved, fill the Cup that Clears
To-day of past Regrets and future Fears—
To-morrow?— Why To-morrow I may be
Myself with Yesterday's Sevn Thousand Years.

— : o : —

Here with a Loaf of Bread beneath the Bough,
A Flask of Wine, a Book of verse – and Thou
Beside me singing in the Wilderness—
And Wilderness is Paradise enow.

— : o : — "Umar Khayyam"

State :— The State presupposes a public power of coercion seperated from the aggregate body of its members. (Engels) PP.116

Origin of State :— .... Degeneration of the old feuds between tribes a regular mode of existing by systematic plundering on land and sea for the purpose of acquiring cattle, slaves and treasures. In short wealth is praised and respected as the highest treasure, and the old gentile institutions are abused in order to justify the forcible robbery of wealth. Only one thing was missing: an institution that not only secured the newly acquired property of private individuals against the communistic traditions of the gens, that not only declared as sacred the formerly so despised private property and represented the protection of this sacred property as the highest purpose of human society, but that also stamped the gradually developing new forms of acquiring property of constantly increasing wealth with the universal sanction of the society. An institution

P.T

Jail Diary-11

"Ah, my Beloved, fill the cup that clears
Today of past Regrets and future Fears —
Tomorrow?- Why tomorrow I may be
Myself with yesterday's Sev'n Thousand Years.

: * :

Here with a loaf of Bread beneath the Bough,
A flask of Wine, a Book of Verse and Thou
Beside me singing in the Wilderness —
And Wilderness is Paradise now!"

Umar Khayyam

STATE

The state presupposes a public power of coercion separated from the aggregate body of its members.

ORIGIN OF STATE

...Degeneration of the old feuds between tribes — a regular mode of existing by systematic plundering on land and sea for the purpose of acquiring cattle, slaves and treasures. In short, wealth is praised and respected as the highest treasure, and the old gentile institutions are abused in order to justify the forcible robbery of wealth. Only one thing was missing: an institution that not only secured the newly acquired property of private individuals against the communistic tradition of the gens, that not only declared as sacred the formerly so despised private property and represented the protection of this sacred property as the highest purpose of human society, but that also stamped the gradually developing new forms of acquiring property of constantly increasing wealth with the universal sanction of the society. An institution

Origin of the State :— that lent the character of perpetuity not only to the newly rising division into classes, but also to the right of the possessing classes to exploit and rule the non-possessing classes.

And this institution was found. The State arose.

pp 129—130.

Definition of Government} "Good government can never be a substitute for self- government."

"Henry Campbell Bannerman"

"We are convinced that there is only one form of Government, whatever it may be called, namely, where the ultimate control is in the hands of the people"

"Earl of Balfour"

Religion} "My own view of religion is that of Lucretius. I regard it as a disease born of fear, and as source of untold misery to the human race. I can not however deny that it has made some contributions to civilization. It helped in early days to fix the calendar and it caused the Egyptian priest to chronicle eclipses with such care that in time they became able to predict them. These two services I am prepared to acknowledge, but I do not know of any other."

Bertrand Russell

ORIGIN OF STATE (Contd)

that lent the character of perpetuity not only to the newly rising divisions into classes, but also to the right of the possessing classes to exploit and rule the non-possessing classes.

And this institution was sound. The state arose.

—: * :—

DEFINITION OF A GOOD GOVERNMENT

"Good government can never be a substitute for self-government."

—Henry Campbell Bannerman

"We are convinced that there is only one form of government, whatever it may be called, namely where the ultimate control is in the hands of the people."

—Earl of Balfour

RELIGION

"My own view of religion is that of Lucretius. I regard it as a disease born of fear and as a source of untold misery to the human race. I cannot, however, deny that it has made some contributions to civilisation. It helped in early days to fix the calendar and it caused the Egyptian priest to chronicle eclipses with such care that in time they became able to predict them. These two services I am prepared to acknowledge, but I do not know of any other."

—Bertrand Russell

Benevolent despotism.

Montague Chelmsford called the British Government a 'benevolent despotism' and according to Ramsay Macdonald, the imperialist leader of the British Labour Party, in all attempts to govern a country by a 'benevolent despotism', the governed are crushed down. They become subjects who obey, not citizens who act. Their literature, their art, their spiritual expression go.

Govt. of India.

Mr. Edwin S. Montague, Secretary of State for India, said in the House of Commons in 1917:—

"The Government of India is too wooden, too iron, too inelastic, too antediluvian, to be of any use for modern purposes. The Indian Govt. is indefensible."

British Rule in India.

Dr. Rutherford's words:—

"British Rule as it is carried on in India is the worst and most immoral system of government in the world — the exploitation of one nation by another."

Liberty & English People.

"The English people love liberty for themselves. They hate all acts of injustice, except those which they themselves commit. They are such liberty-loving people that they interfere in the Congo and cry 'shame' to the Belgians. But they forget their heels are on the neck of India."

An Irish Author

BENEVOLENT DESPOTISM

Montague-Chelmsford called the British Government a 'benevolent despotism' and according to Ramsay Macdonald, the imperialist leader of the British Labour Party, in all attempts to govern a country by a 'benevolent despotism', the governed are crushed down. 'They become subjects who obey; not citizens who act. Their literature, their art, their spiritual expression go.'

———: * :———

GOVT. OF INDIA

Rt. Hon'ble Edwin S. Montague, Secretary of State for India said in the House of Commons in 1917: "The Government of India is too wooden, too iron, too inelastic, too antidiluvian, to be of any use for modern purposes. The Indian Government is indefensible."

BRITISH RULE IN INDIA

Dr Ruthford's words: "British rule as it is carried on in India is the lowest and most immoral system of government in the world — the exploitation of one nation by another."

LIBERTY AND ENGLISH PEOPLE

"The English people love liberty for themselves. They hate all acts of injustice, except those which they themselves commit. They are such liberty-loving people that they interfere in the Congo and cry 'shame' to the Belgians. But they forget their heels are on the neck of India."

— An Irish author

Mob Retaliation

. . . Let us therefore examine how man came by the idea of punishing in this manner.

They learn it from the Governments they live under, and retaliate the punishment they have been accustomed to behold. The heads stuck upon spikes, which remained for years upon Temple Bar, differed nothing in the horror of the scene from those carried about upon spikes at Paris; yet this was done by the English Govt. It may perhaps be said that it signifies nothing to a man what is done to him after he is dead; but it signifies much to the living; it either tortures their feelings or hardens their hearts, and in either case it instructs them how to punish when power falls into their hands. . . .

✓ Lay then the axe to the root, and teach Governments humanity. It is their sanguinary punishments which corrupt mankind. . . . The effect of those cruel spectacles exhibited to the populace is to destroy tenderness or excite revenge; and by the base and false idea of governing men by terror instead of reason, they become precedents.

[Rights of Man. PP. 32, T. Paine]

MOB RETALIATION

...Let us, therefore, examine how men came by the idea of punishing in this manner.

They learn it from the governments they live under, and retaliate the punishment they have been accustomed to behold. The heads stuck upon spikes, which remained for years upon Temple Bar, differed nothing in the horror of the scene from those carried about upon spikes at Paris; yet this was done by the English government. It may perhaps be said that it signifies nothing to a man what is done to him after he is dead; but it signifies much to the living — it either tortures their feelings or hardens their hearts, and in either case, it instructs them how to punish when power falls into their hands.

Lay them the axe to the root and teach governments humanity. It is their sanguinary punishments which corrupt mankind...The effect of those cruel spectacles exhibited to the populace is to destroy tenderness or excite revenge, and by the base and false idea of governing men by terror instead of reason, they become precedents.

Monarch and Monarchy :—

It was not against Louis XVI; but against despotic principles of government, that the Nation revolted. The principles had not their origin in him, but in the original establishment, many centuries back, and they were become too deeply rooted to be removed, and the Augean stable of parasite and plunderers too abominably filthy to be cleansed, by anything short of a complete revolution. When it becomes necessary to do a thing, the whole heart and soul should go into the measure, or not attempt it . . . . The Monarch and the Monarchy were distinct and seperate things; and it was against the person or principles of the former, that the revolt commenced and the Revolution has been carried.

PP. 19.

: o :

Natural & Civil rights :—

Man did not enter enter into society to become worse than he was before, but to have those rights better secured. His natural rights are the foundation of all his civil rights.

Natural rights are those which appertain to man in right of his existence. (intellectual - mental etc.)

Civil rights are those that appertain to man in right of his being a member of society.

PP. 44

: o :

MONARCH AND MONARCHY

It was not against Louis XVI but against despotic principles of government, that the nation revolted. The principles had not their origin in him, but in the original establishment, many centuries back, and they had become too deeply rooted to be removed, and the Augean stable of parasite(s) and plunderers too abominably filthy to be cleansed by anything short of a complete revolution. When it becomes necessary to do a thing, the whole heart and soul should go into the measure, or not attempt it.... The monarch and the monarchy were distinct and separate things; and it was against the person or principles of the former, that the revolt commenced and the revolution has been carried.

——————— : * : ———————

NATURAL AND CIVIL RIGHTS

Man did not enter into society to become worse than what he was before, but to have those rights better secured. His natural rights are the foundation of all his civil rights.

Natural rights are those which appertain to man in right of his existence (intellectual, mental, etc.)

Civil rights are those that appertain to man in right of his being a member of society.

.6 King's Salary:—

It is inhuman to talk of a million sterling a year paid out of the public taxes of any country, for the support of an individual, whilst thousands who are forced to contribute thereto, are pining with want and struggling with misery. Govt. does not consist in a contrast between prisons and palaces, between poverty and pomp; it is not instituted to rob the needy of his mite and increase the wretchedness of the wretched.

P. 204

: o :

"Give me liberty or death"

"It is in vain, sir, to extenuate the matter. Gentlemen, may cry, peace, peace — but there is no peace. The war is actually begun. The next gale that sweeps from the north to our ears the clash of resounding arms. Our brethren are already in the field. Why stand we here idle? What is it that gentlemen wish? What would they have? Is life so dear or peace so sweet as to be purchased at the price of chains and slavery. Forbid it, almighty God! I know not what course other may take. as for me, give me liberty or death."

Patrick Henry.

: o :

Right of labour. — "Whoever produces anything by weary labour, does not need a revelation from heaven to teach him that he has a right to the thing produced."

Robert G. Ingersoll

KING'S SALARY

It is inhuman to talk of a million sterling a year, paid out of the public taxes of any country, for the support of an individual, whilst thousands who are forced to contribute thereto, are paining with want and struggling with misery. Government does not consist in a contract between prisons and palaces, between poverty and pomp; it is not instituted to rob the needy of his mite and increase the worthlessness of the wretched.

———————— : * : ————————

"GIVE ME LIBERTY OR DEATH"

"It is, in vain, sir, to extenuate the matter. Gentlemen may cry, peace, peace, but there is no peace. The war has actually begun. The next gale that sweeps from the North brings to our ears the clash of resounding arms. Or brethren are already in the field. Why stand we here idle? What is it that gentlemen wish? What would they have? Is life so dear or peace so sweet as to be purchased at the price of chains and slavery? Forbid it, Almighty God! I know not what course others may take. As for me, give me liberty or death."

— Patrick Henry

———————— : * : ————————

RIGHT OF LABOUR

"Whoever produces anything by weary labour does not need revelation from heaven to teach him that he has a right to the thing produced."

— Rober G. Ingersoll

"We consider it horrible that people should have their heads cut off, but we have not been taught to see the horror of life-long death which is inflicted upon a whole population by poverty and tyranny." Mark Twain

---

Anarchists.

" . . . . The Anarchists and the apostles of insurrection are also represented; and if some of the things seem to the reader the mere unchaining of furies, I would say, let him not blame the faithful anthologist, let him not blame even the writer — let him blame himself, who has acquiesced in the existence of conditions which have driven his fellowmen to extremes of madness and despair."

Upton Sinclair - Preface 19
Cry for Justice

The Old Labourer.

" . . . He (the old labourer out of employment) was struggling against age, against nature, against circumstances; the entire weight of society, law and order pressed upon him to force him to lose his self-respect and liberty. . . . He knocked at the doors of the farms and found good in man only — not in law and order, but in individual man alone."

Richard Jefferies. 80.

"We consider it horrible that people should have their heads cut off, but we have not been taught to see the horror of lifelong death which is inflicted upon a whole population by poverty and tyranny."

Mark Twain

———————: * :———————

ANARCHISTS

...The Anarchists and the apostles of insurrection are also represented; and if mere some of the things seem to the reader the mere unchaining of furies, I would say, let him not blame the faithful anthologist, let him not blame even the writer — let him blame himself, who has acquiesced in the existence of conditions which have driven his fellowmen to extremes of madness and despair."

— Upton Sinclair, Preface
Cry for Justice

———————: * :———————

THE OLD LABOURER

"...He (the old labourer out of employment) was struggling against age, against nature, against circumstances; the entire weight of society, law and order pressed upon him to lose his self-respect and liberty.... He knocked at the doors of the farmers and found one good man only – not in law and order, but in individual man alone."

— Richard Jefferies

8

Poor Labourers:

"... And we, the men who braved this task, were outcasts of the world. A blind fate, a vast merciless mechanism, cut and shaped the fabric of our existence. We were men despised when we were most useful, rejected when we were not needed, and forgotten when our troubles weighed upon us heavily. We were the men sent out to fight the spirit of the wastes, rob it of all its primeval horrors, and batter down the barriers of its world-old defences. Where we were working a new town would spring up some day; it was already springing up, and then, if one of us walked there, 'a man with no fixed address,' he would be taken up and tried as a loiterer and vagrant."

{From Children of the Dead End
by Patrick Macgill.
C.S. 48.

Morality:—

"Morality and religion are but words for him who fishes in gutters for the means of sustaining life, and crouches behind barrels in the street for shelter from the cutting blasts of a winter night."

Horace Greeley. 128

Hunger

"It is desirable for a ruler that no man should suffer from cold and hunger under his rule. Man can not maintain his standard of morals when he has no ordinary means of living."

Kenko Hoshi Buddhist Monk
of Japan 14th Century
P. 135

POOR LABOURERS

"... .And we, the men who braved this task, were outcasts of the world. A blind fate, a vast merciless mechanism, cut and shaped the fabric of our existence. We were men despised when we were most useful, rejected when we were not needed, and forgotten when our troubles weighed upon us heavily. We were the men sent out to fight the spirit of the wastes, rob it of all its primeval horrors and batter down the barriers of its world-old defences. Where we were working, a new town would spring up some day; it was already springing up, and then, if one of us walked there, 'a man with no fixed address', he would be taken up and tried as a loiterer and vagrant."

— by Patrick Macgill. C. J.,
from Children of the Dead End

: * :

MORALITY

"Morality and religion are but words to him who fishes in gutters for the means of sustaining life, and crouches behind barrels in the street for shelter from the cutting blasts of a winter night."

— Horace Greeley

: * :

HUNGER

"It is desirable for a ruler that no man should suffer from cold and hunger under his rule. Man cannot maintain his standard of morals when he has no ordinary means of living."

— Konko Hoshi, Buddhist monk of
Japan, 14th century

: * :

Freedom :— 19

Men! whose boast it is that ye
Come of fathers, brave and free,
If there breathe on earth a slave,
Are ye truly free and brave?
If you do not feel the chain
When it works a brother's pain,
Are ye not base slaves indeed,
Slaves unworthy to be freed?

Is true Freedom but to break
Fetters for our own dear sake,
And, with leathern hearts, forget
That we owe mankind a debt?
No! True Freedom is to share
All the chains our brothers wear,
And, with heart and hand, to be
Earnest to make others free!

They are slaves who fear to speak
For the fallen and the weak;
They are slaves who will not choose
Hatred, scoffing and abuse,
Rather than in silence shrink
From the truth they needs must think;
They are slaves who dare not be
In the right with two or three.

"James Russell Lowell"

P. 189

FREEDOM

Men! Whose boast it is that ye
Come of fathers, brave and free,
If there breathes on earth a slave,
Are ye truly free and brave?
If you do not feel the chain
When it works a brother's pain,
Are ye not base slaves indeed.
Slaves unworthy to be freed?
Is true Freedom but to break
Fetters for our own dear sake,
And, with leathern hearts, forget,
That we owe mankind a debt?
No! True Freedom is to share
All the chains our brothers wear,
Earnest to make others free!
They are slaves who fear to speak
For the fallen and the weak;
They are slaves who will not choose
Hatred, scoffing and abuse,
Rather than in silence shrink
From the truth they need must think;
They are slaves who dare not be
In the right with two or three.

— James Russel Lowell

: * :

20

Full many a gem of purest ray serene
The dark unfathomed caves of ocean bear;
Full many a flower is born to blush unseen,
And waste its sweetness on the desert air.

: o :

Invention:

Hitherto it is questionable if all the mechanical inventions yet made have lightened the day's toil of any human being.

J. S. Mill P. 199

: o :

Alms:

"There is no one on earth more disgusting and repulsive than he who gives alms. Even as there is no one so miserable as he who accepts them."

Maxim Gorky.
P. 204

: o :

Liberty:

Those corpses of youngmen,
Those martyrs that hang from the gibbets—
those hearts pierced by the grey lead,
Cold and motionless as they seem, live elsewhere
with unslaughter'd vitality.
They live in other youngmen, O kings!
They live in brothers again ready to defy you!
They were purified by death — they were taught
and exalted.

Full many a gem of purest ray serene
The dark unfathomed caves of ocean bear;
Full many a flower is born to blush unseen,
And waste its sweetness on the desert air.

: * :

INVENTION

Hitherto it is questionable if all the mechanical inventions yet made have lightened the day's toil of any human being.

— J.S. Mill

ALMS

"There is no one on earth more disgusting and repulsive than he who gives alms. Even as there is no one so miserable as he who accepts them."

— Maxim Gorky

: * :

LIBERTY

Those corpses of youngmen,
Those martyrs that hang from the gibbets,
Those hearts pierced by the grey lead,
Cold and motionless as they seem, live elsewhere
With unslaughter'd vitality.

They live in other youngmen, O kings!
They live in other brothers again ready to defy you!
They were purified by death – they
Were taught and exalted!

Not a grave of the murder'd for freedom,
but grows seed for freedom, in its turn to bear seed,
Which the wind carry afar and re-sow, and the
rains and the snows nourish.
Not a disembodied spirit can the weapons of tyrants
let loose,
But it stalks invisibly over the earth, whispering,
counselling, cautioning.

P. 268 "Walt Whitman"

Free Thought

"If there is anything that cannot bear
free thought let it crack."
Wendell Phillips 271

State :—

"Away with the state! I will take part
in that revolution. Undermine the whole
conception of a state, declare free choice
and spiritual kinship to be the only all
important conditions of any union, and
You will have the commencement of a
liberty that is worth something."

Henrik Ibsen. 273

Oppression :—

"Surely oppression maketh a wise
man mad."

P. 274

Not a grave of the murder'd for freedom,
But grows seed for freedom, in its turn to bear seed.
Which the wind carry afar and re-sow and the
Rains and the snows nourish.
Not a disembodied spirit can the weapons of tyrant let loose
But it stalks invincibly over the earth, whispering,
Counselling, cautioning.

"Walt Whitman"

—————— : * : ——————

FREE THOUGHT

"If there is anything that cannot bear free thought, let it crack."

— Wendell Phillips

—————— : * : ——————

STATE

"Away with the State! I will take part in that revolution. Undermine the whole conception of a state, declare free choice and spiritual conceptionship to be the only all-important condition of any union, and you will have the commencement of a liberty that is worth something."

— Henrik Ibsen

—————— : * : ——————

OPPRESSION

"Surely oppression maketh a wise man mad."

22

Martyrs!

The man who flings his whole life into attempt, at the cost of his own life, to protest against the wrongs of his fellow-men, is a saint compared to the active and passive upholders of cruelty and injustice, even if his protest destroys other lives besides his own. Let him who is without sin in society cast the first stone at such an one. P. 280

: 0 :

Lower Class

While there is a lower class, I am in it.
While there is a criminal element, I am of it.
While there is a soul in jail, I am not free.

Eugene V. Debs.

164

One against all — [Charles Fourier 1772-1837]

The present social order is a ridiculous mechanism, in which portions of the whole are in conflict and acting against the whole. We see each class in society desire, from interest, the misfortune of the other classes, placing in every way individual interest in opposition to public good. The lawyer wishes litigation and suits, particularly among the rich; the physician desires sickness. (The latter would be ruined if everybody died without disease, as the latter would the former if all quarrels were settled by arbitration.) The soldier wants a war, which will carry off half of his comrades and secure him promotion; the undertaker wants burials; monopolists and forestallers want famine, to double or treble the price of grain; the architect, the carpenter, the mason, want conflagration, that will burn down a hundred houses to give activity to their branches of business.

P. 202

MARTYRS

The man who flings his whole life into an attempt, at the cost of his own life, to protest against the wrongs of his fellowmen, is a saint compared to the active and passive upholders of cruelty and injustice, even if his protest destroys other lives besides his own. Let him who is without sin in society cast the first stone at such a one.

LOWER CLASS

While there is a lower class, I am in it.
While there is a criminal element, I am in it.
While there is a soul in jail, I am not free

— Eugene B. Debs

: * :

ONE AGAINST ALL

[Charles Fourier: 1772-1837]

The present social order is a ridiculous mechanism, in which portions of the whole are in conflict and acting against the whole. We see each class in society desire, from interest, the misfortune of the other classes, placing in every way individual interest in opposition to public good. The lawyer wishes litigation and suits, particularly among the rich; the physician desires sickness. (The latter would be ruined if everybody died without disease, and the former if all quarrels were settled by arbitration). The soldier wants a war, which will carry off half of his comrades and secure him promotion; the undertaker wants burials; monopolists and forestallers want famine, to double or treble the price of grain; the architect, the carpenter, the mason want conflagration that will burn down a hundred houses to give activity to their branches of business.

: * :

New gospel

"Society can overlook murder, adultery or swindling; it never forgives the preaching of a new gospel." P.327 Frederic Harrison

Tree of liberty

The tree of liberty must be refreshed from time to time with the blood of patriots and tyrants. It is its natural manure.

Thomas Jefferson. 332

Chi. Martyrs:—

Say, then, that the man erred grievously; if his error had been ten times as great, it ought to have been wiped from human recollection by his sacrifice. . . .

Granted freely that their idea of the best manner of making a protest was utterly wrong and impossible, granted that they went not the best way to work. But what was it that drove them into attack against the social order as they found it? They and thousands of other men that stood with them were not bad men, nor bloodthirsty, nor hardhearted, nor criminal, nor selfish, nor crafty. Then what was it that made them so bitter and desperate. . . .

No one ever contemplated the simple fact that men do not band themselves together to make a protest without the belief that they have something to protest about, and that in any organized state of society a widespread protest is something for grave inquiry.

Charles Edward Russell. 333.

NEW GOSPEL

"Society can overlook murder, adultery or swindling; it never forgives the preaching of new gospel."

— Frederic Harrison

: * :

TREE OF LIBERTY

The tree of liberty must be refreshed from time to time with the blood of patriots and tyrants. It is natural manure.

— Thomas Jefferson

: * :

CHICAGO MARTYRS

Say, then, that the man erred grievously; if his error had been ten times as great, it ought to have been wiped from human recollection by his sacrifice...

Granted freely that their idea of the best manner of making a protest was utterly wrong and impossible, granted that they went not the best way to work. But what was it that drove them into attack against the social order as they found it? They and thousands of other men that stood with them were not bad men, nor depraved, nor blood-thirsty, nor hard-hearted, nor criminal, nor selfish, nor crazy. Then what is that evoked a complaint so bitter and deep-seated...

No one ever contemplated the simple fact that men do not bend themselves together to make a protest without the belief that they have something to protest about, and that, in any organised state of society, a widespread protest is something for grave inquiry.

— Charles Edward Russell

: * :

24 Will of Revolu

"I also wish my friends to speak little or not at all about me, because idols are created when men are praised, and this is very bad for the future of the human race. Acts alone, no matter by whom committed, ought to be studied, praised or blamed. Let them be praised in order that they may be imitated when they seem to contribute to the common weal; let them be censured when they are regarded as injurious to the general well being, so that they may not be repeated.

I desire that on no occasion, whether near or remote, nor for any reason whatsoever, shall demonstrations of a political or religious character be made before my remains, as I consider the time devoted to the dead would be better employed in improving the condition of the living, most of whom stand in great need of this."

Will of Francisco Ferrer.
Spanish educator 1859-1909
Executed after the Barcelona Riots by a plot of his clerical enemies.

: • :

Charity:—

"Come follow me", said Jesus Christ to the rich young man... To stay in his own set and invest his fortune in work of charity, would have been comparatively easy. Philanthropy has been fashionable in every age. Charity takes the insurrectionary edge off of poverty. Therefore the philanthropic rich man is a benefactor to his fellow magnates, and is made to feel their gratitude; to him all doors of fashion swing. He denied the legitimacy of alms-giving as a plaster for the deep-lying sore in social tissue... Philanthropy as a substitute for justice — he would have none of it...

WILL OF A REVOLUTIONARY

"I also wish my friends to speak little or not at all about me, because idols are created when men are praised, and this is very bad for the future of the human race.... Acts alone, no matter by whom commited, ought to be studied, praised or blamed. Let them be praised in order that they may be initiated when they sided to contribute to the common weal; let them be censured when they are regarded as injurious to the general well-being, so that they may not be repeated.

"I desire that on no occasion, whether near or remote, nor for any reason whatsoever, shall demonstrations of a political or religious character be made before my remains, as I consider the time devoted to the dead would be better employed in improving the conditions of the living, most of whom stand in great need of this."

Will of Franscisco Ferrer
Spanish Educator, 1859-1909
Executed after the Barcelona riots
by a plot of his clerical enemies.

: * :

CHARITY

"Come follow me," said Jesus to a rich young man... To stay in his own set and invest his fortune in work of charity would have been comparatively easy. Philanthrophy has been fashionable in every age. Charity takes the insurrectionary edge off poverty. Therefore, the philanthropic rich man is a benefactor to his fellow magnates, and is made to feel their gratitude; to him all doors of fashion swing. He denied the legitimacy of alms-giving as a plaster for the deep-lying sore in social tissue... Philanthropy as a substitute for justice – he would have none of it...

Charity is twice cursed — it hardens him that gives and softens him that takes. It does more harm to the poor than exploitation, because it makes them willing to be exploited. It breeds slavishness which is moral suicide. The only thing Jesus would permit a swollen fortune to do was to give itself to revolutionary propaganda, in order that swollen fortunes might be forever after impossible...

Bouck White — Clergyman
P. 353 — Born 1874 U.S.A.

Fight for Freedom

The power of armies is a visible thing
Formal, and circumscribed in time and space;
But who the limits of that power shall trace
Which a brave people into light can bring
Or hide, at will, — for freedom combating
By just revenge inflamed? No foot may chase,
No eye can follow, to a fatal place
That power, that spirit, whether on the wing
Like the strong wind, or sleeping like the wind
Within its awful caves — from year to year
Spring this indigenous produce far and near;
No craft this subtle element can bind,
Rising like water from the soil, to find
In every nook a lip that it may cheer.

{W. Wordsworth.}

Charity is twice cursed; it hardens him that gives and softens him that takes. It does more harm to the poor than exploitation, because it makes them willing to be exploited. It breeds slavishness which is moral suicide. The only thing Jesus would permit a swollen fortune to do was to give itself to revolutionary propaganda, in order that swollen fortunes might be forever after impossible...

Bouck White, Clergyman,
Born 1874, USA

———————— : * : ————————

FIGHT FOR FREEDOM

The power of armies is a visible thing
Formal, and circumscribed in time and space;
But who the limits of that power shall trace
Which brave people into light can bring
Or hide, at will, for freedom combating.
By just revenge inflamed? Not foot may chase,
No eye can follow, to a fatal place
That power that spirit whether on the wing
Like the strong wind, or sleeping like the wind.
Within its awful caves – from year to year
Spring this indigenous produce far and near;
No craft this subtle element can bind,
Rising like water from the soil, to find
In every nook a lip that it may cheer.

{W. Wordsworth}

———————— : * : ————————

26 **The Charge of the Light Brigade**

Half a league, half a league,
Half a league onward,
All in the valley of Death
Rode the Six hundred.
'Forward the Light Brigade!
Charge for the guns!' He said;
Into the valley of Death
Rode the six hundred.

"Forward the Light Brigade!'
Was there a man dismayed?
Not, though the soldiers knew
Some one had blundered:

Their's not to make reply,
Their's not to reason why,
Their's but to do and die:
Into the valley of Death
Rode the six hundred.
Cannon to the right of them,
Cannon to the left of them,
Cannon in front of them,
Volleyed and thundered;

Stormed at with shot and Shell,
Boldly they rode and well,
Into the jaws of Death,
Into the mouth of Hell'
Rode the Six Hundred.
Flashed all their sabres bare,
Flashed as they turned in air
Sabring the gunners there,
Charging an army, while
All the world wondered:

Jail Diary-26

THE CHARGE OF THE LIGHT BRIGADE

Half a league, half a league,
Half a league onward,
All in the valley of Death
Rode the six hundred.
"Forward the Light Brigade!
Charge for the guns!" he said;
Into the valley of Death
Rode the six hundred.
"Forward the Light Brigade!"
Was there a man dismayed?
Not, though the soldiers knew
Someone had blundered:
Their's not to make reply,
Their's not to reason why;
Their's but to do and die;
Into the valley of Death
Rode the six hundred.
Cannon to the right of them,
Cannon to the left ot them,
Cannon in front of them,
Volleyed and thundered.
Stormed at with shot and shell,
Boldly they rode and well,
Into the jaws of Death,
Into the mouth of Hell,
Rode the six hundred.
Flashed all their sabres bare,
Flashed as they turned in air
Sabring the gunners there,
Charging army, while
All the world wondered.

Plunged in the battery-smoke
Right through the line they broke,
Cossacks and Russians
Reeled from the sabre stroke
Shattered and sundered.
Cannon to the right of them,
Cannon to the left of them,
Cannon behind them
Volleyed and thundered;
Stormed at with shot and shell,
While horse and hero fell,
They that had fought so well
Came through the jaws of Death,
Back from the Mouth of Hell,
All that was left of them,
Left of six hundred.
When can their glory fade?
O the wild charge they made!
All the world wondered.
Honour, the charge made!
Honour, the Light Brigade!
Noble six hundred.

— Lord Tennyson!

دل دے تو اس مزاج کا پروردگار دے
جو غم کی گھڑی کو بھی خوشی سے گزار دے

چھیڑ نہ اے فرشتے تو ذکرِ غمِ جانانہ
کیوں یاد دلاتے ہو بھولا ہوا افسانہ

Jail Diary-27

Plunged in the battery-smoke
Right through the line they broke,
Cossacks and Russians
Reeled from the sabre stroke
    Shattered and sundered,
Cannon to the right of them,
Cannon to the left of them,
Cannon behind them
    Volleyed and thundered.
Stormed at with shot and shell,
While horse and hero fell,
They that had fought so well
Came through the jaws of Death,
Back from the mouth of Hell,
All that was left of them,
    Left of six hundred.
When can their glory fade?
O the wild charge they made!
All the world wondered.
Honour, the charge made
Honour, the Light Brigade!
    Noble six hundred.
    — Lord Tennyson

: * :

Dil de to is mizaaj kaa parvardigaar de
Jo gham ki ghari ko bhi khushi se guzaar de
(Give me a heart of such disposition, O God
That it may pass the moment of sorrow as it passes happy moments.)

: * :

Sajaa kar mayyiat-i-ummeed naakaami ke phoolon se
Kisi hamdard ne rakh di mere toote hue dil mein.
(Having bedecked may bier of hope with the flowers of failure
Some sympathiser has placed it in my broken heart.)

: * :

سجا کر میّتِ امید ناکامی کے پھولوں سے
کسی بیدرد نے رکھ دی مرے ٹوٹے ہوئے دل میں +

Birth-right

We're the sons of sires that baffled
Crowned and mitred tyranny;
They defied the field and scaffold
For their birth-rights — so will we!

[J. Campbell]

Glory of the cause

Ah! not for idle hatred, not
for honour, fame, nor self applause,
But for the glory of the cause,
You did, what will not be forgot.

[Arthur Clough]

Immortality of Soul:—

For you know if you can once get a man believing in immortality there is nothing more left for you to desire; you can take everything in the world he owns — you can skin him alive if you please — and he will bear it with perfect good humor.

[Upton Sinclair C.J. 403]

For tyrants

A tyrant must put on the appearance of uncommon devotion to religion. Subjects are less apprehensive of illegal treatment from a ruler whom they consider god-fearing and pious. On the other hand, they do less easily move against him, believing that he has the gods on his side. —

Jail Diary-28

Chher naa ae farishte! tu zikr-i-ghame-i-jaanaanaan!
Kyon yaad dilaate ho bhulaa hua afsaanaa!
(Don't start O Angel with the sad story of the dear one!
Why should you remind (me) of that forgotten thing?)

———— : * : ————

BIRTHRIGHT

We're the sons of sires that battled
Crowned and mirted tyranny;
They defied the field and scaffold
For their birthrights — so will we!

— J. Campbell

———— : * : ————

GLORY OF THE CAUSE

Ah! not for idle hatred, not
For honour, fame, nor self-applause,
But for the glory of the cause,
You did, what will not be forgot.

— Arthur Clogh

———— : * : ————

IMMORTALITY OF SOUL

For you know if you can once get a man believing in immortality, there is nothing more left for you to desire; you can take everything in the world he owns, you can skin him alive if you please, and he will bear it with perfect good humour.

— Upton Sinclair, 403 C.J.

———— : * : ————

GOD'S TYRANTS?

A tyrant must put on the appearance of uncommon devotion to religion. Subjects are less apprehensive of illegal treatment from a ruler whom they consider god-fearing and pious. On the other hand, they do less easily move against him, believing that he has the gods on his side.

Soldiers & Thought

If my soldiers were to begin to reflect, not one of them would remain in the ranks.

[Frederick the Great] 582

The noblest fallen

The noblest have fallen. They were buried
obscurely in a deserted place.
No tears fell over them.
Strange hands carried them to the grave.
No cross, no enclosure, and no tomb stone tell
their glorious names.
Grass grows over them; a feeble blade
bending low keeps the secret.
The sole witness were the surging waves,
which furiously beat against the shore.
But even they the mighty waves, could
not carry farewell greetings to the
distant home.

[V. N. Figner]

Prison

'There were no stars, no earth, no time,
No check, no change, no good, no crime,
But silence, and a stirless breath,
Which neither was of life nor death:

[The Prisoner of Chillon]

SOLDIERS AND THOUGHT

If my soldiers were to begin to reflect, not one of them would remain in the ranks.

— Frederick the Great

: * :

THE NOBLEST FALLEN

The noblest have fallen. They were buried
obscurely in a deserted place.
No tears fell over them.
Strange hands carried them to the grave.
No cross, no enclosure, and no tombstone tell
their glorious names.
Grass grows over them, a feeble blade
bending low keeps the secret.
The sole witnesses were the surging waves,
which furiously beat against the shore,
But even they the mighty waves could
not carry farewell greetings to the distant home.

— V.N. Finger

: * :

PRISON

There were no stars, no earth, no time,
No check, no change, no good, no crime,
But silence, and a stirless breath,
Which neither was of life nor death.

— The Prisoner of Chillon

: * :

30

After conviction:—

During the moments which immediately follow upon his sentence, the mind of the condemned in many respects resembles that of a man on the point of death. Quiet, and as if inspired, he no longer clings to what he is about to leave, but firmly looks in front of him, fully conscious of the fact that what is coming is inevitable.

[V. N. Figner]

The Prisoner:—

'It is suffocating under the low, dirty roof;
My strength grows weaker year by year:
They oppress me, this stony floor,
This iron chained table,
This bed stead, this chair, chained
To the walls, like boards of the grave.
In this eternal, dumb, deep silence
One can only consider oneself a corpse.'

"N. A. Morozov."

Nacked walls, prison thoughts,
How dark and sad you are!
How heavy to live a prisoner inactive,
And dream of years of freedom.

[Morozov]

تجھے ذبح کرنے کی خوشی اور مجھے مرنے کا شوق ۔ میری بھی مرضی وہی جو میرے صیاد کی ہے۔

AFTER CONVICTION

During the moments which immediately follow upon his sentence, the mind of the condemned in many respects resembles that of a man on the point of death. Quiet, and as inspired, he no longer clings to what he is about to leave, but firmly looks in front of him, fully conscious of the fact that what is coming is inevitable.

— V.N. Figner

———————— : * : ————————

THE PRISONER

It is suffocating under the low, dirty roof;
My strength grows weaker year by year;
They oppress me, this stony floor,
This bed-stead, this chair, chained
To the walls, like boards of the grave,
In this eternal, dumb, deep silence
One can only consider oneself a corpse.

— N.A. Morozov

———————— : * : ————————

Naked walls, prison thoughts,
How dark and sad you are,
How heavy to be prisoner inactive,
And dream of years of freedom.

— Morozov

———————— : * : ————————

Tujhe zabaah karne ki khushi, mujhe marne kaa shauq
Meri bhi marzi wahi hai, jo mere sayyaad ki hai.
(You derive pleasure in slaughtering,
and I have a craving for dying!
I have the same wish as of my killer.)

31

'Everything here is so silent, lifeless, pale,
The years pass fruitless, leaving no trace.
The weeks and days drag on heavily,
Bringing only dull boredom in their suite.'

[Morozov]

: ° :

Our thoughts grow dull from long confinement;
There is a feeling of heaviness in our bones;
The minutes seem eternal from torturing pain,
In this cell, four steps wide.

: ° :

'Entirely for our fellow men we must live,
Our entire selves for them we must give,
And for their sakes struggle against ill fate!'

[Morozov]

: ° :

Came to set me free .. —

At last men came to set me free;
I ask'd not why, and reck'd not where,
It was at length the same to me,
Fetter'd or fetterless to be:
I learn'd to love despair.
And thus when they appear'd at last,
And all my bonds aside were cast,
These heavy walls to me had grown
A hermitage — and all my own.

[The Prisoner of Chillon]

: ° :

Jail Diary-31

Everything here is so silent, lifeless, pale,
The years pass fruitless, leaving no trace;
The weeks and days drag on heavily,
Bringing only dull boredom in their suite.

— Morozov

: * :

Our thoughts grow dull from long confinenment;
There is a feeling of heaviness in our bones;
The minutes seem eternal from torturing pain,
In this cell, four steps wide.
Entirely for our fellowmen we must live,
Our entire selves for them we must give,
And for their sake, struggle against ill fate!

— Morozov

: * :

CAME TO SET ME FREE

At last men came to set me free;
I ask'd not why and reck'd not where,
It was at length the same to me,
Fetter'd or fetterless to be;
I learn'd to love despair.
And thus when they appeared at last,
And all my bonds aside were cast,
These heavy walls to me had grown
A hermitage – and all my own.

—The Prisoner of Chillon

: * :

32

'And from on high we have been honoured with a mission!
We passed a severe school, but acquired higher knowledge.
Thanks to exile, prison, and a bitter lot,
We know and value the world of truth and freedom!'

[Prisoner of Schlusselburg]

: o :

Death & suffering of a child:

'A child was born. He committed consciously neither bad nor good actions. He fell ill, suffered much and long, until he died in terrible agony. Why? Wherefore? It is the eternal riddle for the philosopher.'

: o :

Frame of mind of a revolutionary:

'He who has ever been under the influence of the life of Jesus, who has borne, in the name of an ideal, humiliation, suffering and death; he who has once considered Him as an ideal and his life as the prototype of a disinterested love, — will understand the frame of mind of the revolutionary who has been sentenced and thrown into a living tomb for his work on behalf of popular freedom." [Vera N. Figner]

: o :

Rights: — Don't ask for rights. Take them. And don't let anyone give them to you. A right that is handed to you for nothing has something the matter with it. It's more than likely it is only only a wrong turned

And from on high we have been honoured with a mission!
We passed a severe school, but acquired higher knowledge.
Thanks to exile, prison, and a bitter lot,
We know and value the world of truth and freedom.

(Prisoner of Schlusselburg)

—: * :—

DEATH AND SUFFERING OF A CHILD

A child was born. He committed consciously neither bad nor good actions. He fell ill, suffered much and long, until he died in terrible agony. Why? Wherefore? It is the eternal riddle for the philosopher.

—: * :—

FRAME OF MIND OF A REVOLUTIONARY

He who has ever been under the influence of the life Jesus, who has born, in the name of an ideal, humiliation, suffering and death; he who has once considered Him as an ideal and His life as the prototype of a disinterested love, will understand the frame of mind of the revolutionary who has been sentenced and thrown into a living tomb for his work on behalf of popular freedom.

(Vera N. Figner)

—: * :—

RIGHTS

Don't ask for rights. Take them. And don't let anyone give them to you. A right that is handed to you for nothing has something that matter with it. It's more than likely, it is only a wrong turned inside out.

—: * :—

No enemies? 33

You have no enemies, you say?
Alas! my friend, the boast is poor;
He who has mingled in the fray
Of duty, that the brave endure,
Must have made foes! If you have none,
Small is the work that you have done.
You've hit no traitor on the hip,
You've dashed no cup from perjured lips,
You've never turned wrong to right,
You've been a coward in the fight.

[Charles Mackay. 74]

Child labour

No fledgling feeds the father bird,
No chicken feeds the hen;
No kitten mouses for the cat —
This glory is for men

We are the wisest, strongest Race —
Loud may our praise be sung!
The only animal alive
That lives upon its young!

[Charlotte Perkins Gilman.] 66

[illegible]

Jail Diary-33

NO ENEMIES?

You have no enemies, you say?
Alas! my friend, the boast is poor;
He who has mingled in the fray
Of duty, that the brave endure,
Must have made foes! If you have none,
Small is the work that you have done.
You've dashed no cup from perjured lip,
You've never turned wrong to right,
You've been a coward in the fight.

Charles Mackay

—————— : * : ——————

CHILD LABOUR

No fledgling feeds the father bird,
No chicken feeds the hen,
No kitten mouses for the cat,
This glory is for men.
We are the wisest, strongest race.
Loud may our praise be sung!
The only animal alive
That lives upon its young!

Charlotte Perking Gilman

—————— : * : ——————

(Torn)

34

No Classes! No Compromise!!

[George D. Herron]

Under the Socialist movement there is coming a time, and the time may be even now at hand, when improved conditions or adjusted wages will no longer be thought to be an answer to the cry of labour; yes when these will be but an insult to the common intelligence. It is not for better wages, improved capitalist conditions or a share of capitalist proffits that the Socialist movement is in the world; it is here for the abolition of wages and profits, and for the end of capitalism and the private capitalist. Reformed political institutions, boards of arbitration between capital and labour, philanthropies and privileges that are but the capitalists' gifts — none of these can much longer answer the question that is making the temples, thrones and Parliaments of the nations tremble. There can be no peace between the man who is down and the man who builds on his back. There can be no reconciliation between classes; there can only be the end of classes. It is idle to talk of good will until there is first justice, and idle to talk of justice until the man who makes the world possesses the work of his own hands. The cry of this world's workers can be answered with nothing save the whole product of their work.

[George D. Herron]

NO CLASSES! NO COMPROMISE!!

Under the socialist movement, there is coming a time, and the time may be even now at hand, when improved conditions or adjusted wages will no longer be thought to be an answer to the cry of labour; yes, when these will be but an insult to the common intelligence. It is not for better wages, improved capitalist conditions or a share of capitalist profits that the socialist movement is in the world; it is here for the abolition of wages and profits, and for the end of capitalism and the private capitalist. Reformed political institutions, boards of arbitration between capital and labour, philanthropies and privileges that are but the capitalist's gifts — none of these can much longer answer the question that is making the temples, thrones and parliaments of the nations tremble. There can be no peace between the man who is down and the man who builds on his back. There can be no reconciliation between classes; there can only be an end of classes. It is idle to talk of goodwill until there is first justice, and idle to hands. The cry of the world's workers can be answered with nothing save the whole product of their work.

George D. Herson

: * :

35

Wastes of Capitalism

Economic Estimates et al.
Austria by Theodore Hertzka (1886)

Every family = 5 roomed 40ft sq. House
to last for 50 years.

Workers' workable age 16—50.

So we have 5,000,000

Labour of 615,000 workers is sufficient to produce food for
22,000,000 people = 12.3% of labo

Including labor cost of transport, luxuries need
only 315,000 [= 6.3%] workers' labour.

that amounts to this that 20% of the available
labour is enough for supporting the whole of
the continent. The rest 80% is exploited
and wasted due to Capitalist order of
Society.

WASTES OF CAPITALISM

Economic estimate about Australia by Theodore Hertzka (1886)

Every family = 5-roomed 40 ft. sq. house
to last for 50 years.

Worker's workable age: 16-50.

So, we have 5,000,000.

Labour of 615,000 workers is sufficient to produce
food for 22,000,000 people = 12.3% of labour.

Including labour cost of transport, luxuries need only

315,000 = 6.33% worker's labour.

That amounts to this that 20% of the available labour is enough for supporting the whole of the continent. The rest 80% is exploited and wasted due to capitalist order of society.

36

Czarist Regime & the Bolshevist Regime:—

Frazier Hunt tells that in the first fourteen months of their rule, the Bolsheviks executed 4,500 men, mostly for stealing and speculation.

After the 1905 Revolution, Stolypin, minister of Czar, caused the execution of 32,[illegible] men within twelve months

[P. 390 Brown check]

CZARIST REGIME AND THE BOLSHEVIST REGIME

Frazier Hunt tells that in the first fourteen months of their rule, the Bolsheviks executed 4,500 men, mostly for stealing and speculation.

After the 1905 Revolution, Stolypin, minister of Czar, caused the execution of 32,773 men within twelve months.

Brass Check

: * :

Permanency of the social institutions. — 81

"It is one of the illusions of each generation that the social institutions in which it lives are, in some peculiar "sense," "natural," unchangeable and permanent. Yet for countless thousands of years social institution have been successively arising, developing, decaying and becoming gradually superseded by others better adapted to contemporary needs.....

... The question, then, is not whether our present civilization will be transformed, but how it will be transformed.

It may, by considerate adaptation, be made to pass gradually and peacefully into a new form. Or, if there is angry resistance instead of adaptation, it may crash, leading mankind painfully to build up a new civilization from the lower level of a stage of social chaos and disorder in which not only the abuses but also the material, intellectual and moral gains of the previous order will have been lost.

P.1. Decay of
Cap. Civilization

—— : o : ——

PERMANENCY OF THE SOCIAL INSTITUTIONS

It is one of the illusions of each generation that the social institutions in which it lives are, in some peculiar sense, 'natural', unchangeable and permanent. Yet, for countless thousands of years, social institutions have been successively arising, developing, decaying and becoming gradually superseded by others better adapted to contemporary needs... The question, then, is not whether our present civilisation will be transformed, but how will it be transformed?

It may, by considerate adaptation, be made to pass gradually and peacefully into a new form. Or, if there is angry resistance instead of adaptation, it may crash, leaving mankind painfully to build up a new civilisation from the lower level of a stage of social chaos and disorder, in which not only the abuses but also the material, intellectual and moral gains of the previous order will have been lost."

— P.I. Decay of Cap. Civilisation

———————— : * : ————————

38

Capitalism & Commercialism !

Rabindranath's address to an assembly of Japanese Students: -

" You had your own industry in Japan; how scrupulously honest and true it was, you can see by its products — by their grace and strength, their conscientiousness in details, where they can hardly be observed. But the tidal wave of falsehood has swept over your land from that part of the world where business is business, and honesty is followed merely as the best policy. Have you never felt shame when you see the trade advertisements, not only plastering the whole town with lies and exaggerations, but invading the green fields, where the peasants do their honest labour, and the hilltops, which greet the first pure light of the morning? .... This commercialism with its barbarity of ugly decorations is a terrible menace to all humanity, because it is setting up the ideal of power over the perfection. It is making the cult of self-seeking exult in its naked shamelessness.... Its movements are violent, its noise is discordantly loud. It is carrying its own damnation because it is trampling into distortion

CAPITALISM AND COMMERCIALISM

Rabindranath's address to an assembly of Japanese students:

You had your own industry in Japan; — how scrupulously honest and true it was, you can see by its products — by their grace and strength, their conscientiousness in details where they can hardly be observed. But the tidal wave of falsehood has swept over your land from that part of the world where business and honesty is followed merely as the last policy. Have you never felt shame when you see the trade advertisements, not only plastering the whole town with lies and exaggerations, but invading the green fields, where the peasants do their honest labour, and to hilltops which greet the first pure light of the morning? . . . This commercialism with its barbarity of ugly decorations is a terrible menace to all humanity because it is setting up the ideal of power over the perfection. It is making the cult of self-seeking exult in its naked shamelessness. Its movements are violent, its noise is discordantly loud. It is carrying its own damnation because it is trampling into distortion.

(contd.)

the humanity upon which it stands. It is strenuously turning out the money at the cost of happiness... The vital ambition of the present civilization of Europe is to have the exclusive possession of the devil.

Capitalist Society

"The foremost truth of political economy is that everyone desires to obtain individual wealth with as little sacrifice as possible."

"Nassau Senior."

---

the humanity upon which it stands.

It is strenuously turning out money at the cost of happiness . . . . The vital ambition of the present civilisation of Europe is to have the exclusive possession of the devil.

: * :

CAPITALIST SOCIETY

The foremost truth of political economy is that everyone desires to obtain individual wealth with as little sacrifice as possible.

— Nassan Senior

: * :

10

Karl Marx on
Religion :—

Man makes religion; religion does not make man. Religion indeed is the self-consciousness and the self-feeling of man who either has not yet found himself, or else (have found himself) has lost himself once more. But man is not an abstract being, squatting down somewhere outside the world. Man is the world of men, the state, society. This state, this society produces religion, produces a perverted world consciousness, because they are a perverted world. Religion is the generalized theory of this world, its encyclopaedic compend, its logic in a popular form ... The fight against religion is, therefore a direct campaign against the world whose spiritual aroma is religion. ...

KARL MARX ON RELIGION

Man makes religion; religion does not make man. Religion, indeed, is the self-consciousness and the self-feeling of man who either has not yet found himself, or else (has found himself) has lost himself once more. But man is not an abstract being squatting down somewhere outside the world. Man is the world of men, the state, society. This state, this society produces religion, produces a perverted world consciousness because they are a perverted world. Religion is the generalised theory of this world, its encyclopaedic compend, its logic in a popular form . . . The fight against religion is, therefore, a direct campaign against the world whose spiritual aroma is religion.

(Contd.)

Continued from last page :—

Religion is the sigh of oppressed
creature, the feelings of a heartless world,
just as it is the spirit of unspiritual
conditions. It is the opium of the people."

The people cannot be really happy
until it has been deprived of illusory
happiness by the abolition of religion. The
demand that the people should shake
itself free of illusion as to its own condition
is the demand that it should abandon
a condition which needs illusion.

The weapon of criticism cannot replace
the criticism of weapons. Physical force must
be overthrown by physical force; but theory,
too, becomes a physical force as soon
as it takes possession of the masses.

Jail Diary-41

Religion is the sigh of oppressed creature, the feeling of a heartless world just as it is the spirit of unspiritual conditions. It is the opium of the people.

The people cannot be really happy until they have been deprived of illusory happiness by the abolition of religion. The demand that the people should shake itself free of illusion as to its own condition is the demand that it should abandon a condition which needs illusion.

The weapon of criticism cannot replace the criticism of weapons. Physical force must be overthrown by physical force; but theory, too, becomes a physical force as soon as it takes possession of the masses.

42

A Revolution not Utopian

A radical revolution, the general emancipation of mankind, is not a utopian dream for Germany; what is utopian is the idea of a partial, an exclusively political revolution, which would leave the pillars of the house standing.

"Great are great because
We are on knees.
Let us Rise!"

A REVOLUTION NOT UTOPIAN

A radical revolution, and general emancipation of mankind, is not a utopian dream for Germany; what is utopian is the idea of a partial, and exclusively political revolution, which would leave the pillars of the house standing.

Great are great because
we are on knees.
Let us rise!

43

Herbert Spencer on State:—

"Whether it be true or not that man was born in iniquity and conceived in sin, it is certainly true that Government was born of aggression and by aggression."

Man & mankind:—

"I am a man, and all that affects mankind concerns me."

Roman Dramatist

England's condition reviewed:—

"Good people, things will never go well in England so long as goods be not in common, and so long as there be villains and gentlemen. By what right are they, whom we call lords, greater folk than we? On what grounds have they deserved it? Why do they hold us in serfage? If we all come of the same father and mother, Adam and Eve, how can they say or prove that they are greater are better than we? If it be not that they make us gain for them by our toil what they spend in their pride. They are clothed in velvet and are warm in their furs and ermines, while we are covered with rags. They have wine and spices and fair bread; and we oatcake, and straw, and water to drink. They have leisure and fine houses; we have pain and labour, the rain and wind in the fields, and yet it is of our toil that these men hold their state."

— of Wat Taylor's Rebel

HERBERT SPENCER ON STATE

Whether it be true or not that man was born in equity and conceived in sin, it is certainly true that government was born of aggression and by aggression."

——————— : * : ———————

MAN AND MANKIND

I am a man, and all that

affects mankind concerns me.

Roman dramatist

——————— : * : ———————

ENGLAND'S CONDITION REVIEWED

Good poeple, things will never go well in England, so long as goods be not in common, and so long as there be villains and gentlemen. By what right are they, whom we call lords, greater folk than we? On what grounds have they deserved it? Why do they hold us in serfage? If we all come of the same father and mother, Adam and Eve, how can they say cr prove that they are greater or are better than we? If it be not that they make us gain for them by our toil what they spend in their pride. They are clothed in velvet and are warm in their furs and ermines, while we are covered with rage. They have wine and spices and their bread; and we eat cake, and straw, and water to drink! They have leisure and fine houses; we have pain and labour, rain and wind in the fields, and yet it is of our toil that these men hold their state. . . .

(Page torn)

44

Revolution & classes

All classes striving for power are revolutionary, and talk of Equality. All classes, when they get into power, are conservative and are convinced that equality is an iridescent dream. All classes but one — the Working Class, for as Comte has said, "The working class is not properly speaking, a class at all, but constitutes the body of society." But the day of the working class, the fusion of all useful people, has not yet even arrived." P.47

"World History for workers" by Alfred Barton.

REVOLUTION AND CLASSES

All classes striving for power are revolutionary, and talk of equality. All classes, when they get into power, are conservative and are convinced that equality is an indecent dream. All classes but one – the working class, for as Comte has said, "The working class is not, properly speaking, a class at all, but constitutes the body of society." But the day of the working class, the fusion of all useful people, has not even yet arrived.

World History for Workers

by Alfred Barton

45

Sir Henry Maine has said.

"That most of the lands of England has passed to its present owners by the mistake of lawyers — mistakes that in lesser criminals were punished by hanging."

"The law convicts the man or woman
Who steals the goose from off the Common,
But lets the greater felon loose
Who steals the Common from the goose."

Sir Henry Maine has said:

"The most of the land of England has passed to its present owners by the mistake of lawyers — mistakes that in lesser criminals were punished by hanging."

———————— : * : ————————

"The law convicts the man or woman
Who steals the goose from the Common,
But lets the greater felon loose
Who steals the Common from the goose."

———————— : * : ————————

46

Democracy :—

Democracy is theoratically a system of political and legal equality. But in concrete and practical operation it is false, for there can be no equality, not even in politics and before the law, so long as there is glaring inequality in economic power. So long as the ruling class owns the workers' jobs and the press and the schools of the country and all organs for the moulding and expression of public opinion; so long as it monopolise all trained public functionaries and disposes of unlimited funds to influence elections, so long as the laws are made by the ruling class and the courts are presided over by members of that class; so long as lawyers are private practitioners who sell their skill to the highest bidder, and litigation is technical and costly, so long will the nominal equality before the law be a hollow mockery.

In a capitalist regime the whole machinery of democracy operates to keep the ruling-class minority in power through the sufferage of the working class majority, and when the bourgeois govt feels itself endangered by democratic institutions, such institutions are often crushed without compunction.

P. 58.
"From Marx to Lenin"
(by Morris Hillquit)

Democracy does not secure "equal rights and a share in all political rights for everybody, to whatever class or party he may belong." (Kautsky) It only allows free political and legal play for the existing economic inequalities... Democracy under Capitalism is thus not general, abstract democracy but specific bourgeois democracy;—or as Lenin terms it—democracy for the Bourgeois.

Jail Diary-46

DEMOCRACY

Democracy is theoretically a system of political and legal equality. But in concrete and practical operation it is false, for there can be no equality, not even in politics and before the law, so long as there is glaring inequality in economic power. So long as the ruling class owns the worker's jobs and press and the schools of the country and all organs of the moulding and expression of public opinion; so long as it monopolises all trained public functionaries and disposes off unlimited funds to influence elections; so long as the laws are made by the ruling class and the courts are presided over by members of the class; so long as lawyers are private practitioners who sell their skill to the highest bidder, and litigation is technical and costly, so long will the nominal equality before the law be a hollow mockery.

In a capitalist regime, the whole machinery of democracy operates to keep the ruling class minority in power through the sufferage of the working class majority, and when the bourgeois government feels itself endangered by democratic institutions, such institutions are often crushed without compunction.

From Marx to Lenin
by Morris Hillquiet

———————— : * : ————————

Democracy does no secure "equal rights and a share in all political rights for everybody, to whatever class or party he may belong." (Kautsky). It only allows free political and legal play for the existing economic inequalities . . . Democracy under capitalism is thus no general, abstract democracy but specific bourgeois democracy, . . . or as Lenin terms it — democracy for the bourgeois.

(Page torn)

"Term "Revolution" defined":—

"The conception of revolution is not to be treated in the police interpretation of the term, in the sense of an armed rising. A party would be mad that would choose the method of insurrection on principle so long as it has at its disposal different, less costly and safer methods of action. In that sense social democracy was never revolutionary on principle. It is so only in the sense that it recognizes that when it attains political power it can not employ it for any purpose other than the abolition of the mode of production upon which the present system rests."

"~~[illegible]~~"

"Karl Kautsky.

Some facts and figures, about ~~England~~ United States

5 men can produce bread for 1000
1 man " " cotton cloth for 250
1 man " " woollens for 300
1 man " " boots & shoes 1000

F.M. [illegible]

15,000,000 are living abject poverty who can't even maintain their working efficiency.
3,000,000 Child labourers

Re: England:—

Prewar estimates!

Total Production of England (per annum) £ 2,000,000,000
Gains through foreign investments £ 200,000,000
£ 2,200,000,000

1/9th part of the population took away 1/2 i.e. £ 1100,000,000
2/9th " " 1/3 of the Rest £ 1100,000,000
i.e. £ [illegible]00,000,000

2/3 [illegible] " "

TERM REVOLUTION DEFINED

The conception of revolution is not to be treated in the police interpretation of the term, in the sense of an armed rising. A party would be mad that would choose the method of insurrection on principle so long as it has at its disposal different, less costly, and safer methods of action. In that sense, social democracy was never revolutionary on principle. It is so only in the sense that it recognises that when it attains political power, it cannot employ it for any purpose other than the abolition of the mode of production upon which the present system rests.

— Karl Kautsky

———————: * :———————

SOME FACTS AND FIGURES ABOUT UNITED STATES

5 men can produce bread for 1000
1 man can produce woollens for 300
1 man can produce boots and shoes for 1000

Iron Heel p.

———————: * :———————

15,000,000 are living under abject poverty who cannot even maintain their working efficiency.
3,000,000 child labourers.

———————: * :———————

RE: ENGLAND

Pre-war estimates!

Totol production of England (per annum)	£ 2000,000,000
Gains through foreign investments	£ 200,000,000
	£ 220,000,000

1/9th part of the population took away

1/2 = £1100,000,000

2/9 part of the population 1/3 of the rest = £1100,000,000

(Page torn)

48

Internationale

Arise, ye prisoners of starvation!
Arise ye wretched on earth,
For justice thunders "condemnation",
A better world's in birth.
No more traditions chains shall bind us,
Arise, ye slaves! no more in thrall!
The earth shall rise on new foundations,
We have been naught, we be all.

[Refrain]

It is the final conflict,
Let each stand in his place,
The Internationale Party
Shall be the human race.

Behold them seated in their glory
The kings of mine and rail and soil!
What would you read in all their story
But that they plundered toil?
Fruits of people's work are buried
In the strong coffers of a few;
In working for their restitution,
The men will ask only their due.

[Same Refrain]

Toilers from shops and fields united,
The party we of all who work;
The earth belongs to us, the people,
No room here for the shirk.
"How" many on our flesh have fattened!
" But if the noisome birds of prey,
Shall vanish from our sky some morning
The blessed sunlight still will stay.

[Same refrain]

INTERNATIONALE

Arise, ye prisoners of starvation!
Arise ye wretched on earth,
To justice thunders condemnation,
A better word's in birth.
No more tradition chains shall bind us.
Arise, ye slaves! no more in thrall!
The earth shall rise on new foundations,
We have been naught, we be all.
[Refrain]
It is the final conflict,
Let each stand in his place,
The Internationale Party
Shall be the human race.

: * :

Behold them seated in their glory,
The kings of mine and rail and soil!
What would you read in all their story
But how they plundered toil?
Fruits of people's work are buried
In the strong coffers of a few;
In voting for their restitution,
The man will ask only their due.
[Same refrain]
Toilers from shops and fields united,
The party we of all who work;
The earth belongs to us, the people,
No room here for the shirk,
How many on our flesh have fattened?
But if the noisome birds of prey,
Shall vanish from our sky some morning
The blessed sunlight still will stay.
[Same refrain again]

Marseillaise

Ye sons of toil, awake to glory!
Hark, hark, what myriads bid you rise;
Your children, wives and grandsires hoary,
Behold their tears and hear their cries!
Shall hateful tyrants mischief breeding,
With hireling hosts, a ruffian band—
Affright and desolate the land
While peace and liberty lie bleeding?

[Chorus]

To arms, to arms! ye brave!
The avenging sword unsheathe
March on, march on, all hearts resolved
On victory or death.

With luxury and pride surrounded,
The vile insatiate despots dare;
Their thirst for gold and power unbounded
To meet and vend the light and air;
Like beasts of burden would they load us,
Like gods would bid their slaves adore,
But man is man and who is more?
Then shall they longer lash and goad us?

[The same chorus again]

Oh liberty! Can man resign thee,
Once having felt thy generous flame?
Can dungeons bolts and bars confine thee,
Or whips thy noble spirit tame?
Too long the world has wept bewailing,
That falsehoods dagger tyrants wield;
But freedom is our sword and shield,
And all their arts are unavailing?

[Same chorus again]

MARSEILLAISE

Ye sons of toil, awake to glory!
Hark, hark, what myriads bid you rise;
Your children, wives and grand sires having,
Behold their tears and hear their cires!
Shall hateful tyrants mischief breeding,
With hireling hosts, a ruffian band —
Affright and desolate the land
"While peace and liberty lie bleeding?
[Chorus]
To arms, To arms! Ye brave!
The avenging sword unsheathe
March on, march on, all hearts resolved,
On victory or death.
With luxury and pride unsounded,
The vile insatiate despots dare,
Their thirst for gold and power unbounded
To meet and vend the light and air;
Like beasts of burden would they load us,
Like gods would bid their slaves adore,
But man is man and who is more?
Then shall they longer last and goad us?
[The same chorus again]
Oh liberty! Can man resign thee,
Once having felt thy generous flame?
Can dungeon's bolts and bars confine thee,
Or whips thy noble spirit tame?
Too long the world has wept bewailing.
That falsehood, daggers tyrants wield;
But freedom is our sword and shield,
And all their arts are unavailing?
[Same chorus again]

50

Growth of Opportunism:—

It was the possibility of acting with in law that reared opportunism with in the labour parties of the period of Second Internationale.

[Lenin vid Collapse of II Int. N.]

Illegal work:—

"In a country where the bourgeoisie, or the counterrevolutionary Social-Democracy is in power, the communist party must learn to coordinate its legal work with illegal work, and the legal work must always be under the effective control of the illegal party."

Bukharin

Betrayal of II Int: N.'s cause:—

The vast organization of socialism and labour were adjusted to such peacetime activities, and when the crisis came a number of the leaders and large portion of the masses were unable to adapt themselves to the new situation .... It is this inevitable development that accounts for largely for the betrayal of II Inter National.

Marx to Lenin P. 140
Morris Hillquit.

"The Cynic's Word Book" (1906)

Ambrose Bierce writes:—

"Grape shot— n. An argument which the future is preparing in answer to the demands of American Socialism."

GROWTH OF OPPORTUNISM

It was the possibility of acting within law that reared opportunism within the labour parties of the period of Second Internationale.

[Lenin vide Collapse of II Int. N.]

———————— : * : ————————

ILLEGAL WORK

In a country where the bourgeosie, or the conter-revolutionary Social Democracy is in power, the Communist Party must learn to coordinate its legal work with illegal work, and the legal work must always be under the effective control of the illegal party.

Bukharin

———————— : * : ————————

BETRAYAL OF INT. N.'S CAUSE

The vast organisation of socialism and labour were adjusted to such peace time activities, and when the crisis came, a number of the leaders and large portion of the masses were unable to adopt themselves to the new situation.... It is this inevitable development that accounts largely for the betrayal of II International.

Marx to Lenin

by Morris Hallquiet

———————— : * : ————————

The Cynic's Word Book (1906)

Ambrose Prierce writes:

"Grape shot: An argument which the future is preparing in answer to the demands of American Socialism."

Religion a supporter of the established order: — : 5

Slavery — In 1835 the General Assembly of the Presbyterian Church resolves that: – 'slavery is recognized in both old and new Testaments, and is not condemned by the authority of God."

The Charleston Baptist Association issued the following in 1835:
"The right of masters to dispose of the time of their slaves has been distinctly recognized by the creator of all things, who is surely at liberty to vest the right of property over any object whomsoever He pleases."

The Revd: E. D. Simon Doctor of Divinity a professor in Methodist College of Virginia wrote: —

"Extracts from Holy Writ unequivocally assert the right of property in slaves, together with the usual incidents to that right. The right to buy and sell is clearly stated. Upon the whole, then, whether we consult the Jewish policy instituted by God Himself, or the uniform opinion and practice of mankind in all ages, or the injunctions of the New Testament and the moral law, we are brought to the conclusion that slavery is not immoral. Having established the point that the first African slaves were legally brought into bondage, the right to detain their children in bondage follows as an indispensable consequence. Thus we see that the slavery that exists in America was founded in right."

Capitalism supported — Henry Van Dyke writes in "Essays in Application" (1905)
"The Bible teaches that God owns the world. He distributes to every man according to His own good pleasure, conformably to the general laws."

RELIGION A SUPPORTER OF THE ESTABLISHED ORDER

SLAVERY

In 1835, the General Assembly of the Presbytarian Church resolved that: "Slavery is recognised in both Old and New Testaments, and is not condemned by the authority of God."

The Charleston Baptist Association issued the following is 1835: "The right of masters to dispose of the time of their slaves has been distinctly recognised by the Creator of all things, who is surely at liberty to vest the right of property over any object whomsoever He pleases."

The Revd. E.D. Simon, Doctor of Divinity, a professor in Methodist College of Virginia, wrote:

"Extracts from Holy Writ unequivocally assert the right of property in slaves, together with the usual incidents to that right. The right to buy and sell is clearly stated. Upon the whole, then whether we consult the Jewish policy instituted by God Himself, or the uniform opinion and practice of mankind in all ages, or the injunctions of the New Testament and the moral law, we are brought to the conclusion that slavery is not immoral. Having established the point that the first African slaves were legally bought into bondage, the right to detain their children in bondage follows as an indispensable consequence. Thus, we see that the slavery that exists in America was founded in right."

CAPITALISM SUPPORTED

Henry Van Dyke writes in *"Essay in Application"* (1905):

"The Bible teaches that God owns the world. He distributes to every man according to His own good pleasure, conformably to the general laws."

: * :

12 Statistics about United States.

Army was 50,000 strong }
It is now 300,000 strong }

Plutocracy owns 67 billions of wealth.
Out of the total persons engaged in occupation only $\frac{9}{10}$% belong to Plutocracy yet they own 70% of the total wealth.
Out of Persons engaged in occupations 29% belong to Middle Class.
They own 25% of the total wealth = 24 billions
Remaining 70% of the men in occupations belong to the Proletariat and they only 4% of the total wealth. i.e. 4 billions

According to Lucien Sanial in 1900:—
Out of all People engaged in occupation = 250,251 belonged to Plutocrats
" = 8,429,845 Middle Class
" = 20,393,137 Proletariats

(Iron Heel)

Rifles!

You say you will have majority in the Parliament and State offices, but
"How many rifles have you got? Do you know where you can get plenty of lead? When it comes to powder, the chemical mixtures are better than mechanical mixtures. You take my word."

P. 198 Iron Heel

STATISTICS ABOUT UNITED STATES

Army was 50,000 strong

It is now 300,000 strong.

——————————: * :——————————

Plutocracy owns 67 billions of wealth.
Out of the total persons engaged in occupations only
9/10% belong to plutocracy
Yet they own 70% of the total wealth.
Out of persons engaged in occupations,
29% belong to middle class
They own 25% of the total wealth = 24 billions.
Remaining 70% of the men in occupations belong to
the Proletariat and they only (get)
4% of the total wealth, i.e. 4 billions.
According to Lucian Saniel, in 1900:
Out of total people engaged in occupations = 250, 251
belonged to Plutocrats
" " = 8,429,845 to Middle Class
" " = 20,395,137 to Proletariat

Iron Heel

——————————: * :——————————

RIFLES

You say you will have majority in the Parliament and State offices, but "How many rifles have you got? Do you know where you can get plenty of lead? When it comes to powder, the chemical mixtures are better than mechanical mixtures. You take my word."

Iron Heel

<u>Power & Government.</u> 53

A socialist leader had addressed a meeting of the plutocrats and charged them of mismanaging a society and thereby thrown the whole responsibility on their shoulders, the responsibility for the woes and misery that confronts the suffering humanity. Afterwards a capitalist (Mr. Wickson) rose and addressed him as follows:—

"This, then, is our answer. We have no words to waste on you. When you reach out your vaunted strong hands for our palaces and purpled ease, we will show you what strength is. In roar of shell and shrapnel and in whine of machine guns will our answer be couched. We will grind you revolutionists down under our heel, and we shall walk upon your faces. The world is ours, we are its lords and ours it shall remain. As for the host of labour, it has always been in the dirt since history began, and I read history aright. And in the dirt it shall remain so long as I and mine and those that come after us have the power. There is the word. It is the king of words — Power. Not God, not mammon, but Power. Pour it over your tongue till it tingles with it. Power."

"I am answered," Earnest (the socialist leader) said quietly. "It is the only answer that could be given. Power. It is what we of the working class preach. We know, and well we know by bitter experience that, no appeal for the right, for justice, for humanity can ever touch you. Your hearts are hard as your heels with which you tread upon the faces of the poor. So we have preached power. By the power of our ballots on election day will we take your government away from you ——"

"What if you do get a majority, a sweeping majority on election day," Mr. Wickson broke in to demand. "Suppose we refuse to turn the Govt. over to you after you have captured it at the ballot box?"

POWER TO THE (illegibl, torn)

A socialist leader had addressed a meeting of the Plutocrats and charged them of mismanaging the society and thereby thrown the whole responsibility on their shoulders, the responsibility for the woes and misery that confronts the suffering humanity. Afterwards a capitalist (Mr. Wickson) rose and addressed him as follows:

"This, then, is our answer. We have no words to waste on you. When you reach out your vaunted strong hands for our palaces and purpled ease, we will show you what strength is in roar of shell or will shrapnel and in whine of machine guns will our answer be couched. We will grind you revolutionists down under our heel, and we shall walk upon your faces. The world is ours. We are its lords and ours it shall remain. As for the host of labour, it has always been in the dirt since history began, and I read history aright. And in the dirt it shall remain so long as I and mine, and those that come after us, have the power.

There is the word. It is the king of words — Power, Not God, not mammon, but Power. Pour it over your tongue till it tingles with it. Power."

"I am answered," Earnest (the socialist leader) said quietly. "It is the only answer that could be given. Power, it is what we of the working class preach. We know, and well we know by bitter experience, that no appeal for the right, for justice, for humanity can ever touch you. Your hearts are hard as your heels with which you tread upon the faces of the poor. So we have preached Power. By the Power of our ballots, on election day, will we take your government away from you . . ."

"What if you do get a majority, a sweeping majority on election day," Mr. Wickson broke in to demand. "Suppose we refuse to turn the government over to you after you have captured it at the ballot box?"

(contd.)

54

"That also, have we considered," Ernest replied. "And we shall give you an answer in terms of lead. Power, you have proclaimed the king of words. Very good! Power it shall be. And in the day that we sweep to victory at the ballot box and you refuse to turn over to us the govt. we have constitutionally and peacefully captured, and you demand what we are going to do about it — in that day, I say, we shall answer you; and in roar of shell and shrapnel and in whine of machine-guns shall our answer be couched.

"You can not escape us. It is true that you have read history aright. It is true that labour has from the beginning of history been in the dirt. And it is equally true that so long as you and yours and those that come after you have power, that labour shall remain in the dirt. I agree with you. I agree with all that you have said. Power will be the arbiter, as it always has been the arbiter. It is a struggle of classes. Just as your class dragged down the old feudal nobility, so shall it be dragged down by my class, the working class. If you will read your biology and your sociology as clearly as do your history, you will see that this end I have described is inevitable. It does not matter whether it is in one year, ten or a thousand — your class shall be dragged down. And it shall be done by power. We of the labour host have conned that word over till our minds are all atingle with it. Power. It is a kingly word."

Iron Heel (P.88)
by Jack London

Jail Diary-54

"That also have we considered," Earnest replied. "And we shall give you an answer in terms of lead. Power, you have proclaimed the king of words. Very good! Power, it shall be. And in the day that we sweep to victory at the ballot box, and you refuse to turn over to us the government we have constitutionally and peacefully captured, and your demand what we are going to do about it in that day, I say, we shall answer you; and in roar of shell and sharpnel, in whine of machine guns shall our answer be couched.

"You cannot escape us. It is true that you have read history aright. It is true that labour has, from the beginning of history, been in the dirt. And it is equally true that so long as you and yours and those that come after you, have power, that labour shall ramain in the dirt. I agree with you. I agree with all that you have said. Power will be the arbiter, as it always has been the arbiter. It is a struggle of classes. Just as your class dragged down the old feudal nobility, so shall it be dragged down by my class, the working class. If you will read your biology and your sociology as clearly as do your history, you will see that this end I have described is inevitable. It does not matter whether it is in one year, ten or a thousand — your class shall be dragged down. And it shall be done by power. We of the labour host have conned that word over, till our minds are all atingle with it. Power. It is a kingly word."

Iron Heel (p. 88)

by Jack London

Figures :—

England :—

1922 — number of unemployment 1,135,000

1926 — it has oscillated b/w $1\frac{1}{4}$ and $1\frac{1}{2}$ millions i.e. 1,250,000 to 1,500,000

Betrayal of the English labour leaders :—

The years 1911 to 1913 were times of unparalleled class struggles of the miners, railwaymen, and transport workers generally. In August 1911 a national, in other words a general, strike broke out on the railways. The vague shadow of revolution hovered over Britain in those days. The leaders exerted all their strength in order to paralyze the movement. Their motive was 'Patriotism'; the affair was occurring at the time of the Agadir incident, which threatened to lead to a war with Germany. As is well known today, the premier summoned the workers' leaders to a secret council, and called them to the salvation of the fatherland. And leaders did all that lay in their power, strengthening the bourgeoisie, and thus preparing the way for an imperialist slaughter.

P. 8.

Crew in Britain Jr. L.D.T.

Jail Diary-55

FIGURES
England:
1922 – Number of unemployed 1,135,000
1926 – it has oscillated to 1¼ and 1½ millions, i.e. 1,250,000 to 1,500,000.

BETRAYAL OF THE ENGLISH LABOUR LEADERS

The years 1911 to 1913 were times of unparalleled class struggles of the miners, railwaymen, and transport workers generally. In August 1911, a national, in other words, a general, strike broke out on the railways. The vague shadow of revolution hovered over Britain in those days. The leaders exerted all their strength in order to paralyse the movement. Their motive was 'patriotism'; the affair was occurring at the time of the Agadir incident, which threatened to lead to a war with Germany. As it is well known today, the Premier summoned the workers' leaders to a secret council, and called them to the salvation of the fatherland. And leaders did all that lay in their power, strengthening the bourgeoisie, and thus preparing the way for the imperialist slaughter.

Where is Britain...

Trotsky

56 **Betrayal** —

It was only after 1920 the movement returned its[*] bounds, after the 'Black Friday' when the Triple alliance of miners', railwaymen's, and transport leaders betrayed the general strike. P. 3

[*] interlinear insertion written above "the movement": "its"

For Reform a threat of revolution is necessary: —

The British bourgeoisie reckoned that by such means (reforms) a revolution could be avoided. It follows, therefore, that even for the introduction of reforms the principle of gradualness alone is insufficient, and that an actual threat of revolution is necessary. P. 28

Social Solidarity!: —

It would seem that once we stand for the annihilation of a privileged class which has no desire to pass from the scene, we have herein the basic content of the class struggle. But no, Macdonald desires to 'evoke' the consciousness of social solidarity. With whom? The solidarity of the working class is the expression of its internal welding in the struggle with the bourgeoisie.

The social solidarity which Macdonald preaches is the solidarity of the exploited with the exploiters, in other words, the maintenance of exploitation.

Revolution a calamity; —

"The revolution in Russia", says Macdonald "taught us a great lesson. It showed that revolution is a ruin and a calamity & nothing more."

(Next Page)

BETRAYAL

Only after 1920 did the movement return within bounds, after 'Black Friday' when the Triple alliance of miners, railwaymen and transport leaders betrayed the general strike.

—————— : * : ——————

FOR REFORM, A THREAT OF REVOLUTION IS NECESSARY

. . . The British bourgeoisie reckoned that by such means, (reform) revolution could be avoided. It follows, therefore, that even for the introduction of reforms, the principle of gradualness alone is insufficient, and that an actual threat of revolution is necessary.

—————— : * : ——————

SOCIAL SOLIDARITY

. . . It would seem that once we stand for the annihilation of a privileged class which has no desire to pass from the scene, we have therein the basic content of the class struggle. But no, Macdonald desires to 'evoke' the consciousness of social solidarity. With whom? The solidarity of the working class is the expression of its internal welding in the struggle with the bourgeoisie.

The social solidarity, which Macdonald preaches, is the solidarity of the exploited with the exploiters in other words, the maintenance of exploitation.

—————— : * : ——————

REVOLUTION A CALAMITY

"The revolution in Russia," says Macdonald, "taught us a great lesson. It showed that revolution is a ruin and a calamity and nothing more."

(contd.)

Revolution leads only to calamity! But the British democracy led to the imperialist war, ... with the ruin of which the calamities of revolution cannot, of course, compared in the very least. But in addition to this, what deaf ears and shameless face are necessary in order in the face of a revolution which overthrew Tsarism, nobility and bourgeoisie shook the Church, awakened to a new life a nation of 130 millions, a whole family of nations; to declare that revolution is ~~nothing~~ a calamity and nothing more.

P. 64.

Peaceful?:—

When and where did the ruling class ever yield power and property on the order of a peaceful vote — and especially such a class as the British bourgeoisie, which has behind it centuries of world rapacity.

P. 66

Aim of Socialism:— Peace

It is absolutely unchallenged that the aim of Socialism is to eliminate force, first of all in its most crude and bloody forms, and afterwards in other more concealed forms.

P. 80

"Where is ~~Brit~~ Britain going?"
Trotsky.

Aim of the World Revolution:—

1. To over throw Capitalism
2. To control the nature for the service of humanity.

This is how Bukharin depicts it.

"Revolution leads only to calamity! But the British Democracy led to the imperialist war . . . . with the ruin of which the calamities of revolution cannot, of course, be compared in the very least. But in addition to this, what deaf ears and shameless faces are necessary in order, in the face of a revolution which overthrew Czarism, nobility and bourgeoisie, shook the church, awakened to a new life a nation of 130 millions, a whole family of nations, to declare that revolution is a calamity and nothing more."

———————— : * : ————————

PEACEFUL?

When and where did the ruling class ever yield power and property on the order of a peaceful vote — and especially such a class as the British bourgeoisie, which has behind it centuries of world rapacity?

———————— : * : ————————

AIM OF SOCIALISM PEACE

It is absolutely unchallenged that the aim of socialism is to eliminate force, first of all in its most crude and bloody forms, and afterwards in other more concealed forms.

Where is Britain Going

Trotsky

———————— : * : ————————

AIM OF THE WORLD REVOLUTION

1. To overthrow capitalism
2. To control the nature for the service of humanity.

* This is how Bukharin has defined it. – Bhagat Singh

58

Man and machinery:—

The United States Bureau of Labour tells:—

12 lbs package of pins can be made by a man working with a machine in 1 hr. 34 minutes.

Ratio: [1½ : 140.55] [illegible] times } The same would take 140 hours and 55 minutes if man works with tools only but without machine.

—— : o : ——

100 pairs of shoes by machine work take 234 hrs 26 min.
By hand it will take 1,831 hrs 40 minutes.
Labour Cost by machine is $ 69.55
" by hand is $ 457.92

—— : o : ——

500 yards of gingham checks are made by machine labour in 73 hours.
By hand labour it takes 5,844 hours.

—— : o : ——

100 lbs of sewing cotton can be made by machine labour in 39 hrs,
by hand it takes 2,895 hours.

Re: Agriculture—

A good man with a scythe can reap 1 acre a day (12 hrs)
A machine does the same work in 20 minutes.
Six men with flails can thresh 60 liters of wheat in half an hour
One machine thresher can do 12 times as much

"The increased effectiveness of man-labour, aided by the use of machinery... varies from 150% in the case of rye, to 2,244% in the case of barley..."

—— : o : ——

MAN AND MACHINERY

The United States Bureau of Labour tells:

12 lbs package of pins can be made by a man working with a machine in 1 hr. 34 minutes. The same would take 140 hours and 55 minutes, if man works with tools only, but without machine.
{Ratio: 1.34 :140.55 times}

100 pairs of shoes by machine work take 234 hrs. 25 min.
By hand it will take 1,831 hrs. 40 minutes.
Labour cost on machine is $69.55
By hand is $457.92

———: * :———

500 yards of gingham checks are made by machine labour in 73 hours.
By hand labour, it takes 5,844 hours.

———: * :———

100 lbs of sewing cotton can be made by machine labour in 39 hours.
By hand labour it takes 2,895 hours.

———: * :———

Re: Agriculture
A good man with a scythe can reap 1 acre a day (12 hrs)
A machine does the same work in 20 minutes
One machine thresher can do 12 times as much.
"The increased effectiveness of man-labour, aided by the use of machinery . . . varies from 150% in the case of rice, to 2,244% in the case of barley . . ."

———: * :———

The wealth of U.S.A. & its Population :—

1850 — 1912

59

	Total wealth was	Per Capita	T. Populn.
In 1850	$ 7,135,780,000 —	$ 308	= 23,191,876
1860	16,159,616,000	$ 514	= 31,443,321
1870	30,068,518,000	$ 780	= 38,558,371
1880	43,642,000,000	$ 870	= 50,155,783
1890	65,037,091,000	$ 1,036	= 62,947,714
1900	88,517,307,000	$ 1,165	= 75,994,575
1904	107,104,202,000	$ 1,318	= 82,466,551
1912	187,139,071,000	$ 1,965	= 95,410,503

Due to the use of machinery.

: o :

The machine is social in nature, as the tool was individual.

"Give us worse cotton, but give us better men" says Emerson.

"Deliver me those rickety perishing souls of infants, and let the cotton trade take its chance."

P. 81

: o :

The man cannot be sacrificed to the machine. The machine must serve mankind, yet the danger to the human race lurks, menacing in the Industrial Regime.

Poverty & Riches P. 81
Scott Nearing

Jail Diary-59

The Wealth of U.S.A. and Its Population: (1850-1912)

In 1850	Total wealth was	Per Capita		T. Population
	$ 7,13,780,000	$ 308	=	23,191,876
1860	$ 16,159,616,000	$ 514	=	1,443,321
1870	$ 30,068,518,000	$ 780	=	38,558,371
1880	$ 43,642,000,000	$ 870	=	50,155,785
1890	$ 65,037,091,000	$ 1,036	=	82,947,714
1900	$ 88,517,307,000	$ 1,165	=	75,994,575
1904	$ 107,104,202,000	$ 1,318	=	82,466,551
1912	$ 187,139,071,000	$ 1,965	=	9,540,503

Due to the use of machinery

———————— : * : ————————

The machine is social in nature, as the toll was individual.

"Given us worse cotton, but give us better men," says Emerson. "Deliver me those rickety perishing souls of infants, and let the cotton trade take its chance."

———————— : * : ————————

The man cannot be scarificed to the machine. The machine must serve mankind, yet the danger to the human race lurks, menacing, in the Industrial regime.

Proverty & Riches,

Scott Nearing

———————— : * : ————————

* Due to the use of machinery. – Bhagat Singh

60

Man and Machinery:—

C. Hanford Henderson, in his "Pay day" writes:

"This institution of industry, the most primitive of all institutions, organized and developed in order to free mankind from the tyranny of things, has become itself the greater tyrant degrading a multitude into the condition of slaves — slaves doomed to produce, through long and weary hours, a senseless glut of things and then forced to suffer for the lack of the very things they have produced."

"Poor: Riches P. 87"

Man is not for machinery

The combination of steel and fire, which man has produced and called a machine, must be ever the servant, never the master of man. Neither the machine nor the machine owner may rule the human race. P. 88.

Imperialism:—

Imperialism is capitalism in that stage of developement in which monopolies and financial capital have attained a preponderating influence, the export of capital has acquired great importance, the international trusts have begun the partition of the world, and the biggest capitalist countries have completed the division of the entire terrestrial globe among themselves."

Lenin.

MAN AND MACHINERY

C. Hanford Henderson, in his *Payday* writes:

"This institution of industry, the most primitive of all institutions, organised and developed in order to free mankind from the tyranny of things, has become itself the greater tyranny of things, degrading a multitude into the condition of slaves — slaves doomed to produce, through long and weary hours, a senseless glut of things and then forced to suffer for the lack of the very things they have produced."

: * :

MAN IS NOT FOR MACHINERY

The combination of steel and fire, which man has produced and called a machine, must be ever the servant, never the master of man. Neither the machine nor the machine owner may rule the human race.

: * :

IMPERIALISM

"Imperialism is capitalism in that stage of development in which monopolies and financial capital have attained a preponderating influence, the export of capital has acquired great importance, the international trusts have begun the partition of the world, and the biggest capitalist countries have completed the division of the entire terrestrial globe among themselves."

: * :

Dictator Ship :—

Dictatorship is an authority relying directly upon force, and not bound by any laws.

The revolutionary dictatorship of the proletariat is an authority maintained by the proletariat by means of force over and against the bourgeoisie, and not bound by any laws.

Prol: Rev: P 18. Lenin

Revolutionary Dictatorship :—

Revolution is an act in which one section of the population imposes its will upon the other by rifles, bayonets, guns, and other such exceedingly authoritarian means. And the party which has won is necessarily compelled to maintain its rule by means of that fear which its arms inspire in the reactionaries. If the Commune of Paris had not relied upon the armed people as against the bourgeoisie, would it have maintained itself more than twenty-four hours? Are we not, on the contrary, justified in reproaching the Commune for having employed this authority too little?"

— F. Engels.

Bourgeois Democracy :—

Bourgeois democracy while constituting a great historical advance in comparison with feudalism, nevertheless remains, and can not but remain, a very limited, a very hypocritical institution, a paradise for the rich and a trap and a delusion for the exploited and for the Poor.

Lenin P. 28.

DICTATORSHIP

Dictatorship is an authority relying directly upon force, and not bound by any laws.

The revolutionary dictatorship of the proletariat is an authority maintained by the proletariat by means of force over and against the bourgeoisie, and not bound by any laws.

———: * :———

REVOLUTIONARY DICTATORSHIP

Revolution is an act in which one section of the population imposes its will upon the other by rifles, bayonets, guns, and other such exceedingly authoritarian means. And the party which has won is necessarily compelled to maintain its rule by means of that fear which its arms inspire in the reactionaries. If the Commune of Paris had not relied upon the armed people as against the bourgeoisie, would it have maintained itself more than twenty-four hours? Are we not, on the contrary, justified in reproaching the Commune for having employed this authority too little?

———: * :———

BOURGEOIS DEMOCRACY

Bourgeois democracy, while constituting a great historical advance in comparison with feudalism, nevertheless, remains, and cannot but remain, a very limited, a very hypocritical, institution, a paradise for the rich and a trap and a delusion for the exploited and for the poor.

———: * :———

62

Exploitation of Labour and State:—

"Not only the ancient and feudal, but also the representative State of today is an instrument of exploitation of wage-labour by capital." Engels.

Dictatorship:—

"Since the state is only a temporary institution which is to be made use of in revolution in order forcibly to suppress the opponents, it is perfectly absurd to talk of about a free popular State, so long as the proletariat still needs the State it needs it not in the interest of freedom, but in order to suppress its opponents, and when it becomes possible to speak of freedom the State, as such, ceases to exist."

Engels in his letter to Babel March 28th 1875.

The impatient idealists:—

The impatient idealists — and without some impatience a man will hardly prove effective — is almost sure to be led into hatred by the oppositions and disappointments which he encounters in his endeavour to bring happiness to the world.

Bertrand Russell.

EXPLOITATION OF LABOUR AND STATE

"Not only the ancient and feudal, but also the representative state of today is an instrument of exploitation of wage-labour by capital."

: * :

DICTATORSHIP

"Since the state is only a temporary institution which is to be made use of in revolution, in order forcibly to suppress the opponents, it is perfectly absurd to talk about a free popular state; so long as the proletariat still needs the state, it needs it not in the interest of freedom, but in order to suppress its opponents, and when it becomes possible to speak of freedom, the state, as such, ceases to exist."

Engels in his letter to Babel

March 28th, 1875

: * :

THE IMPATIENT IDEALISTS

The impatient idealist – and without some impatience, a man will hardly prove effective – is almost sure to be led into hatred by the oppositions and disappointments which he encounters in his endeavour to bring happiness to the world.

Bertrand Russell

: * :

Leader:—

"No time need have gone to ruin" writes Carlyle, "could it have found a man great enough, a man wise and good enough; wisdom to discern truly what the time wanted, valour to lead it on the right road thither; these are the salvation of any time."

Arbitrariness.—

Kautsky had written a booklet with the title "Proletariate Dictatorship" and had deplored the act of Bolsheviks in depriving the bourgeoisie people from the right of vote. Lenin writes in his "Proletarian Revolution":— (PP 77)

Arbitrariness! Only think what a depth of meanest subservience to the bourgeoisie, and of the most idiotic pedantry, is contained in such a reproach. When thoroughly bourgeois and, for the most part, even reactionary jurists of capitalist countries have in the course of, we may almost say, centuries, been drawing up rules and regulations and writing up hundreds of volumes of various codes and laws, and of interpretations of them to oppress the workers, to bind the poor hand and foot, the poor man, and to place a hundred and one hindrances and obstacles in the way of the simple and toiling mass of the people — when this is done the bourgeois Liberals and Mr. Kautsky can see no "arbitrariness"! It is all law & order! It has all been thought out and written down, how the poor man is to be kept down and squeezed. There are thousands and thousands of bourgeois lawyers and officials able to interpret the laws that the worker and average peasant can never break through their barbed wire entanglements. This, of course, is not any arbitrariness this, of course is not a dictatorship of the filthy & profit seeking exploiters who are drinking the blood of the people. Oh, it is nothing of the kind. It is "pure democracy," which is becoming purer and purer

P.T.O.

LEADER

"No time need have gone to ruin," writes Carlyle, "could it have found a man great enough, a man wise and good enough; wisdom to discern truly what the time wanted, valour to lead it on the right road thither; these are the salvation of any time."

———————— : * : ————————

ARBITRARINESS

Kautsky had written a booklet with the title *Proletariat Dictatorship* and had deplored the act of Bolsheviks in depriving the bourgeoisie people from the right of vote. Lenin writes in his *Proletarian Revolution*.

Arbitrariness! Only think what a depth of meanest subserviency to the bourgeoisie, and of the most idiotic pedantry, is contained in such a reproach. When thoroughly bourgeois and, for the most part, even reactionary jurists of capitalist countries, have in the course of, we may almost say, centuries, been drawing up rules and regulations and writing up hundreds of volumes of various codes and laws, and of interpretations of them to oppress the workers, to bind hand and foot the poor men, and to place a hundred and one hindrances and obstacles in the way of the simple and toiling mass of the people — when this is done, the bourgeois Liberals and Mr. Kautsky can see no 'arbitrariness'! It is all Law and Order! It has all been thought out and written down, how the poor thousands and thousands of bourgeois lawyers and officials able to interpret the laws that the worker and average peasant can never break through their barbed wire entanglements. This, of course, is not any arbitrariness. This, of course, is not a dictatorship of the filthy or profit-seeking exploiters who are drinking the blood of the people. Oh, it is nothing of the kind! It is 'pure democracy', which is becoming purer and purer.

(P.T.O.)

every day. But when the toiling and exploited masses for the first time in history, seperated by Imperialist war from their brothers across the frontiers, have constructed their soviets, have summoned to the work of political construction, the classes which the bourgeois used to oppress and to stupefy, and begun themselves to build up a new proletarian State, begun, in the midst of raging battles, in the fire of civil war, to lay down the fundamental principles of a State without exploitation, then all the scoundrels of the bourgeoisie, the entire band of blood suckers, with Kautsky singing obligato, scream about arbitrariness!

(Lenin) P. 7776

Party:—

But it ~~is clear~~ has become clear that no revolution is possible unless there is a party able to lead the revolution. (P. 15. Lessons of October 1917)

A party is the instrument indispensable to a proletarian revolution. (P. 17. ~~Ibid~~ by Trotsky)

Every day. But when the toiling and exploited masses, for the first time in history, separated by Imperialist War from their brothers across the frontier, have constructed their Soviets, have summoned to the workers of political construction, the classes which the bourgeois used to oppress and to stupefy, and begun themselves to build up a new proletarian State, in the midst of raging battle, in the fire of Civil War, to lay down the fundamental principles of a 'State without exploiters', then all the scoundrels of the bourgeoisie, the entire band of blood suckers, with Kautsky, singing 'obliger to', scream about arbitrariness!

: * :

PARTY

But it has become clean that no revolution is possible unless there is a party able to lead the revolution.

(*Lessons of October*)

(1917)

: * :

A party is the instrument indispensable to a proletarian revolution.

(Ibid by Trotsky)

65

12/7/30

Law, morality, religion are ~~text~~ to him (the working man) so many bourgeois prejudices, behind which lurk in ambush just as many bourgeois interests.

Karl Marx — Manifesto

Jail Diary-65

Signed/(B.K. Dutta)

12/7/30
12/7/30

Law, morality, religion are to him (the working man) so many bourgeois prejudices, behind which lurk in ambush just as many bourgeois interests.

Karl Marx, *Manifesto*

* Page 66 is blank.

B K Dutta
12th July '30

Autograph
of Mr. B K Dutta
taken on 12th July '30
in Cell No: 137
Central Jail Lahore,
four days before his final
departure from this Jail.
Bhagat Singh

Jail Diary-67

Signatures (B.K. Dutta)

12th July, 30

Autograph
Of Mr B.K. Dutta
Taken on 12th July, 30
in Cell. No. 137
Central Jail, Lahore,
four days before his final
departure from this jail.

Bhagat Singh

* Page 68 is blank.

Aim of Communists:—

"The communists disdain to conceal their ~~views~~ views and ~~aim~~ aim. They openly declare that their ends can be attained only by the forcible overthrow of all existing social conditions. Let the ruling classes tremble at a Communist revolution. The proletarians have nothing to lose but their chains. They have a world to win. Working men of all countries, unite!"

Aim of Communist Revolution:—

"We have seen above, that the first step in the revolution by the working class, is to raise the proletariat to the position of ruling class, to win the battle of democracy, to wrest, by degrees, all capital from the bourgeoisie, to centralize all instruments of production in the hands of the State, i.e. of the proletariat organized as the ruling class; and to increase the total of productive forces as rapidly as possible.

"Communist Manifesto"

AIM OF COMMUNISTS

"The Communists disdain to conceal their views and aims. They openly declare that their ends can be attained only by the forcible overthrow of all existing social conditions. Let the ruling classes tremble at a Communist revolution. The proletarians have nothing to lose but their chains. They have a world to win. Working men of all countries, unite!"

———————— : * : ————————

AIM OF COMMUNIST REVOLUTION

"We have seen above that the first step in the revolution by the working class is to raise the proletariat to the position of ruling class, to win the battle of democracy, to wrest, by degrees, all capital from the bourgeoisie, to centralise all instruments of production in the hands of the State, i.e. of the proletariat organised as the ruling class, and to increase the total of productive forces as rapidly as possible."

Communist Manifesto

70 To point out the mistakes of Karl Marx :—

... And it certainly looks as if Trotzky belonged to what Germans calls the school of "real politics" and was as innocent as Bismarck of any ideology at all. And it is therefore rather curious to note that even Trotzky is not revolutionary enough to say that Marx had made a mistake, but feels obliged to devote a few pages or so to the task of exegesis—that is, proving that the sacred books meant something quite different from what they said.

{ Preface to The Lessons of October 1917 by Trotsky
Preface by A. Susan Lawrence.

Voice of the People :—

The Govts we know have all ruled, in the main, by indifference of the people; They have always been Govts of a minority, of this or that fraction of the country which is politically conscious. But when the giant wakes he will have his way, and all that matters to the world is whether he will wake in time.

Preface

TO POINT OUT THE MISTAKES OF KARL MARX

...And it certainly looks as if Trotsky belonged to what Germans called the school of "real politics" and was as innocent as Bismarck of any ideology at all. All it is, therefore, rather curious to note that even Trotsky is not revolutionary enough to say that Marx had made a mistake; but feels obliged to devote a page or so to the task of exegesis — that is, proving that the sacred books meant something quite different from what they said.

Preface to the *Lessons of October 1917* by Trotsky
Preface
by A. Susan Lawrence

: * :

VOICE OF THE PEOPLE

The Governments we know have all ruled, in the main, by indifference of the people; they have always been Government of a minority, of this or that fraction of the country which is politically conscious. But when the giant wakes, he will have his way, and all that matters to the world is whether he will wake in time.

Preface

"It too often happens," wrote Lenin in July 1917, "that when events take a sudden turn, even an advanced party cannot adapt itself for some time to the new conditions. It goes on repeating yesterday's watchwords, watchwords which, under the new circumstances, have become empty of meaning and which have lost meaning 'unexpectedly' just in proportion as the change of in events has been 'unexpected'."

Lessons of Oct: P 17

Tactics and Strategy:—

In politics as in war, tactics means the art of conducting isolated operations; strategy means the art of victory, that is the actual seizure of power.

P. 18

Propaganda and action:—

And it is an extremely sudden change, when the party of the Proletariat ~~class~~ passes from preparation, from propaganda and organization and agitation, to an actual struggle for power an an actual insurrection against the bourgeoisie. Those in the party who are irresolute, or sceptical, or compromising, or cowardly ... oppose the insurrection they look for theoratical arguments to justify their opposition, and they find them all ready made, among their opponents of yesterday.

Trotzky

Jail Diary-71

"It so often happens," wrote Lenin in July 1917, "that when events take a sudden turn, even an advanced party cannot adapt itself for some time to the new conditions. It goes on repeating yesterday's watchwords; watchwords which, under the new circumstances, have become empty of meaning and which have lost meaning 'unexpectedly', just in proportion as the change of events has been 'unexpected'."

Lessons of October

——————: * :——————

TACTICS AND STRATEGY

In politics as in war, tactics means the art of conducting isolated operations; strategy means the art of victory, that is the actual seizure of power.

——————: * :——————

PROPAGANDA AND ACTION

And it is an extremely sudden change, when the party of the Proletariat passes from preparation, from propaganda and organisation and agitation, to an actual struggle for power and an actual insurrection against the bourgeoisie. Those in the party who are irresolute, or sceptical, or compromising, or cowardly . . . oppose the insurrection; they look for theoretical arguments to justify their opposition, and they find them, all readymade, [illegible]mong the[illegible]ts of yesterday.

Trotsky

72

"It is necessary to direct ourselves, not by old formulas, but by new realities." Lenin (P 25)

He always fought for the future against the past. 41

... But a moment comes when the habit of thinking that the enemy is stronger becomes the main obstacle to victory. ... Trotzky 48

... But in such circumstances not every party will have its Lenin.

... What does ~~this~~ it mean to lose the moment? ... ...

All the art of tactics consists in this, to snatch the moment when the combination of circumstances is most favourable...

(Circumstances had produced the combination and Lenin said) The crisis must be settled in one way or another. 'Now or never' repeated Lenin.

P. 52

"It is necessary to direct ourselves, not by old formulas, but by new realities."

Lenin

He always fought for the future against the past.

...But a moment comes when the habit of thinking that the enemy is stronger becomes the main obstacle to victory.

Trotsky

—————— : * : ——————

...But in such circumstances, not every party will have its Lenin.

...What does it mean to lose the moment?...

All the art of tactics consists in this, to match the moment when the combination of circumstances is most favourable . . .

(Circumstances had produced the combination and Lenin said). The crisis must be settled in one way or another. 'Now or never', repeated Lenin.

—————— : * : ——————

The strength of a revolutionary party grows to a certain ~~ex~~ point, after which the contrary may happen.

"To hesitate is crime" wrote at the beginning of October, "to wait for the Congress of Soviets is a childish playing with formalities, a disgraceful playing with formalities; it is betraying the revolution."

Opportune moment:—

Time is an important factor in politics; it is thousand times more so in war and revolution. Things can be done today that can not be done tomorrow. To rise in arms, to defeat the enemy, to seize power, may be possible today, and tomorrow may be impossible. But, you will say, to seize power means changing the course of history; is it possible that such a thing can depend on a delay of 24 hrs? Even so. When it comes to an armed insurrection, events are not measured by the long yardstick of politics but by short yards of war. To lose a few weeks, a few days, sometimes even one day, may mean giving up the revolution, may mean capitulation.

Political cunning is always dangerous, especially in a revolution. You may deceive the enemy but you may confuse the masses who are following you

The strength of a revolutionary party grows to a certain point, after which the contrary may happen....

"To hesitate is crime," (Lenin) wrote in the beginning of October, "to wait for the Congress of Soviets is childish, a disgraceful playing with formalities; it is betraying the revolution."

———————: * :———————

OPPORTUNE MOMENT

Time is an important factor in politics; it is thousand times more so in war and revolution. Things can be done today that cannot be done tomorrow. To rise in arms, to defeat the enemy, to seize power may be possible today, and tomorrow, may be impossible. But, you will say, to seize power means changing the course of history; is it possible that such a thing can depend on a delay of 24 hours? Even so, when it comes to an armed insurrection, events are not measured by the long yards of politics but by short yards of war. To lose a few weeks, a few days, sometimes even one day, may mean giving up the revolution, may mean capitulation.

Political cunning is always dangerous, especially in a revolution. You may deceive the enemy, but you may confuse the masses who are following you.

74

Hesitation:—

Hesitation on the part of the leaders, and felt by their followers, is generally harmful in politics; but in the case of an armed insurrection it is a deadly danger.

War:— ... 'War is war'; come what may, there must be no hesitation or loss of time.

The inefficient leaders:—

There are two kinds of leaders who incline to drag the party back at the moment when it should go fastest. One kind always tends to see overwhelming difficulties and obstacles in the way of revolution, and looks at them — consciously or unconsciously — with the desire of avoiding them. They alter Marxism into a system for explaining why revolutionary action is impossible.

The other kind are mere superficial agitators. They see never any obstacles until they break their heads against them. They think they can avoid real ~~differences~~ difficulties by floods of oratory. They look at everything with supreme optimism, and, naturally, change right over when something has actually to be done.

P 88

HESITATION

Hesitation on the part of the leaders, and felt by their followers, is generally harmful in politics; but in the case of an armed insurrection, it is a deadly danger.

——————— : * : ———————

WAR

..."War is war"; come what may, there must be no hestitation or loss of time.

——————— : * : ———————

THE EFFICIENT LEADERS

....There are two kinds of leaders who incline to drag the party back at the moment when it should go fast. One kind always tends to see overwhelming difficulties and obstacles in the way of revolution, and looks at them — consciously or unconsciously — with the desire of avoiding them. They alter Marxism into a system, for explaining why revolutionary action is impossible.

The other kind are mere superficial agitators. They see never any obstacles until they break their heads against them. They think they can avoid real difficulties by floods of oratory. They look at everything with supreme optimism, and, naturally, change right over when something has actually to be done.

* Pages 75 to 100 are blank.

Sociology :-

101

Value :—

"1 quarter corn = x cwt. of iron. What does this equation tell us? It tells us that in two different things — in 1 quarter of corn and x cwt. of iron — there exists in equal quantities, something common to both. The two things must therefore be equal to a third, which in itself is neither the one or the other. . . Let us now consider the residue of each of these products; it consists of the same unsubstantial reality in each, a mere congelation of homogeneous human labour, of labour power expended without regard to the mode of its expenditure. All these things now tell us that human labour-power has been expended in their production, that labour is embodied in them. When looked at as crystals of this social substance, common to all, they are Values."

Marx — "Capital", English Translation PP. 34-5.

✓ Law :—

"Society, however, does not rest upon law. This is a legal fiction. Rather the law must rest on society. It must be the expression of the interest and needs of society which result from the social and invariably material method of production as against the arbitrariness of the individual. As for Napoleonic Code, which I have in my hand, that has not engendered modern Civil Society. The Society which arose in the 18th Century and developed in the 19th, finds in the Code only a legal expression. As soon as that no longer corresponds to social conditions, it is merely so much waste paper. . . . . The laws necessarily changed with the changing conditions of life. The maintaining of the old laws against the new needs and demands of the social development is at bottom nothing but a hypocritical assertion (in accord with the spirit of the age) of special interest against the common interest." Marx. [Before the Court of Jury of Cologne.]

✓ " . . . "

SOCIOLOGY:

Value

"1 quarter corn = x/cost of iron. What does this question tell us? It tells us that in two different things — in 1 quarter of corn and x cost of iron — there exists in equal quantities something common to both. The two things must, therefore, be equal to a third, which in itself is neither the one or the other . . . let us now consider the residue of each of these products; it consists of the same unsubstantial reality in each, a mere congelation of homogenous human labour, of labour power expended without regard to the mode of its expenditure. All these things now tell us that human labour power has been expended in their production, that labour is embodied in them. When looked at as crystals of this social substance, common to all, they are <u>values.</u>"

Marx, *Capital*, English translation

Law

"Society, however, does not rest upon law. This is a legal fiction. Rather, the law must rest on society. It must be the expression of the interest and needs of society which result from the social and invariably material method of production as against the arbitrariness of the individual. As for Napoleon Code, which I have in my hand, that has not engendered modern civil society. The society which arose in the 18th century and developed in the 9th finds in the Code only a legal expression. As soon as that no longer corresponds to social conditions, it is merely so much waste paper . . . The law necessarily changed with the changing conditions of life. The maintaining of the old law against the new needs and demands of the social development is at bottom nothing but a hypocritical assertion (in accord with the spirit of the age) of special interest against the common interest."

Marx, before the Court of Jury, of Colonge

"Masses":—

"The people is a fat and mottley beast, ignorant of its powers and hence enduring burdens, lashes and cudgel. It is driven by a feeble child, whom it can shake off in an instant. But it fears that child and so it serves all its whims and fancies, never realizing how much it itself is feared by that child... Marvelous thing! They hang themselves with their own hands and send themselves to jails and bring upon themselves war and death for a single farthing, paid to them out of the many that they themselves have given to the King. Everything between heaven and earth belongs to them, but they do not know it, and should anyone tell them that, they would knock that man down and kill him." Tommasso Campanella.

102

"Marxism Versus Socialism" by Madimir G. Simkhovitch. Ph.D.
(1908-12) Columbia University.

He criticises all the theories of Marx one by one and refutes all:

1. Theory of Value
2. Economic Interpretation of History
3. Concentration of wealth in fewer hands i.e. the Capitalists and elimination of Middle Class altogether and swarming of the Proletariat Class.
4. Theory of increasing misery leading to the
5. Inevitable Crisis of the Modern State and Social Order.

He concludes that the Marxism solely rests on these fundamental theories and refutes them one by one, concluding that all the vague apprehensions about the sweeping avalanche of the Revolution has proved futile till now. The middle Class is not diminishing but growing. Rich Class is growing in number and the Mode of production and consumption is also changing alongwith the circumstances hence the reforms in the condition of the workers causing any sort of friction. It is not the growing poverty that is the cause of the social unrest but it is the concentration of the poor classes in industrial centres that the Class Consciousness is growing. Hence all this hue and cry.

Masses

"The People is a fat and motley beast, ignorant of its prowess and hence enduring burdens, lash and cudgel, driven it is by a feeble child, whom it can shake off in an instant. But it fears that child and so serves all its whims and fancies, never realising how much it itself is feared by that child...Marvellous thing! They hang themselves with their own hands and send themselves to jails and bring upon themselves war and death for a single farthing, paid to them out of the many that they themselves have given to the King. Everything between heaven and earth belongs to them, but they do not know it, and should anyone tell them that, they would knock that man down and kill him."

— Tommasso Campanella

—————— : * : ——————

MARXISM VERSUS SOCIALISM

(1908-12) Vladimir G. Simkhovitch Ph.D.,
Columbia University

He criticises all the Theories of Marx one by one and refutes all:

1. Theory of value
2. Economic interpretation of History
3. Concentration of Wealth in fewer hands, i.e. the capitalists, and elimination of middle class altogether and swarming of the proletariat class.
4. Theory of increasing misery leading to the
5. Inevitable crises of the modern State and social order.

He concludes that Marxism solely rests on these fundamental theories and refutes them and by one, concluding that all the vague apprehensions about the hurrying avalanche of the Revolution has proved futile till now. The middle class is not diminishing but growing. Rich class is growing in number and the mode of production and consumption is also changing along with circumstances; hence the reforms in the condition of the workers can avoid any suit of friction. It is not the growing poverty that is the cause of the social unrest, but it is the concentration of the poor classes in Industrial Centres that the class consciousness is growing. Hence all this hue and cry.

Preface to Les-Miserables.

So long as there shall exist, by virtue of law and custom a social damnation artificially creating hells in the midst of civilization, and complicating the destiny which is divine with a fatality which is human; so long as three problems of the age — the degradation of man through poverty, the ruin of woman through hunger, the crippling of children through ignorance — are not solved; so long as in certain regions social asphyxia is possible, — in other words, and from a still wider point of view, so long as ignorance and wretchedness exist on the earth, books like this can not be useless.

(suffocation)

"Victor Hugo".

A judge Defined :—

"A judge callous to the pain he inflicts loses the right to judge" "Rabindra Nath Tagore".

—— : o : ——

"But what unresisting martyrdom fails to do, righteous and resisting force does and renders tyranny impotent to do further harm."

—— : 0 : ——

"Rather get killed than converted" was the cry prevalent amongst the Hindus then. But Ramdas rose and exclaimed," No: not thus. 'Better get killed than converted' is good enough: but it would be better so to strive as neither to get killed nor violently converted by killing the forces of violence itself. Get killed if that must be, but get killed while killing to conquer — conquer in the cause of Righteousness.

Hindu Pad Padshahi

(184 Pg.)

PREFACE TO LES' MISERABLES

So long as there shall exist, by virtue of law and custom, a social damnation artificially creating hells in the midst of civilisation, and complicating the destiny which is divine with a fatality which is human; so long as three problems of the age — the degradation of man through poverty, the ruin of woman through hunger, the crippling of children through ignorance — are not solved; so long as in certain regions, social asphyxia[2] is possible — in other words, and from a still wider point of view, so long as ignorance and wretchedness exist on the earth, books like this cannot be useless.

— Victor Hugo

A JUDGE DEFINED

"A judge callous to the pain he inflicts loses the right to judge."

Rabindranath Tagore

: * :

"But what unresisting martyrdom fails to do, righteous and resisting force does and renders tyranny impotent to do further harm."

: * :

"Rather get killed than converted", was the cry prevalent amongst the Hindus then. But Ram Das rose and exclaimed, "No! Not thus! Better get killed than converted" is good enough; but it would be better so to strive as neither to get killed nor violently converted, by killing the forces of violence itself. Get killed if that must be, while killing to conquer — conquer in the cause of Righteousness."

— *Hindu Padpadshahi*

---

2 Suffocation – Bhagat Singh

104

All Legislators defined as criminals

"All legislators and rulers of men commencing with the earliest down to Lycurgus, Solon, Mahomet, Napoleon etc etc have, one and all, been criminals, for, whilst giving new laws, they have naturally broken through old ones which had been faithfully observed by society and transmitted by its progenitors. [Pp 205. Crime & Punishment Doston[?] Heky.

A true politician", says Burke, "always considers how he shall make the most of the existing materials of his country."

Jail Diary-104

ALL LEGISLATORS DEFINED AS CRIMINALS

All legislators and rulers of men commencing with the earliest down to Lycurgus, Solon, Mahomet, Napoleon, etc., have, one and all, been criminals for whilst giving new laws, they have naturally broken through older ones which had been faithfully observed by society and transmitted by its progenitors."

— [P.205, *Crime and Punishment*], Dostoyevsky

—————————— : * : ——————————

"A true politician," says Burke, "always considers how he shall make the most of the existing materials of his country."

Jurisprudence :— 105

Law :—

1. Legal exposition — as it exists.
2. Legal History — As it develops.
3. Science of Legislation — As it ought to be.

—— : o : ——

1. Theoretical } jurisprudence :. Philosophy. Supplying foundation for the science.
2. General }

—— : o : ——

1. Analytical }
2. Historical } jurisprudence
3. Ethical }

1. Analytical jurisprudence explains the first principles of Law. It deals with (a) conception of Civil Law
(b) Relation between Civil & other Laws
(c) Various constituent ideas that constitute the idea of law viz State, sovereignty and administration of justice.
(d) Legal sources of Law and theory of legislation Etc.
(e) Scientific arrangements of Law
(f) Legal rights.
(g) Theory of legal (civil & criminal) liability
(h) Other legal conceptions.

Jurisprudence

Law

1. Legal Exposition	as it exists.
2. Legal History	as it is developed.
3. Science of Legislation	as it ought to be

———————— : * : ————————

1. Theoretical 2. General	(i) Philosophy. Supplying foundation for the Science Jurisprudence

———————— : * : ————————

1. Analytical 2. Historical 3. Ethical	Jurisprudence

(1) Analytical jurisprudence explains the first principles of Law. It deals with:

(a) Conception of Civil Law

(b) Relation between Civil and other Laws

(c) Various constituent ideas that constitute the idea of Law, viz. State Sovereignty and administration of justice.

(d) Legal Sources of Law, and Theory of Legislation, etc.

(e) Scientific arrangements of Law

(f) Legal rights

(g) Theory of legal (civil and criminal) liability

(h) Other legal conceptions.

106

(2) Historical Jurisprudence deals with the general principles governing the origin and development of Law; legal conceptions. It is the history.

(3) Ethical jurisprudence:— is concerned with the theory of justice in its relation to Law.

Law & Justice:- The total disregard of the ethical implications of the Law tends to reduce analytical jurisprudence to a system rather arid formalism.

Do in England — Two different words, 'Law' and 'justice' are a constant reminder that these are two different things and not the same thing. And there use tends to hide from view the real and intimate relation which exists between them.

[Recht = Right : Droit = Law]

& Continent — Continental speech conceals the difference between 'law' and 'right' whereas English speech conceals the connection between them.

Jail Diary-106

(2) Historical Jurisprudence deals with the general principles governing the origin and development of law; legal conceptions. It is the history.

(3) Ethical Jurisprudence is concerned with the theory of justice in its relation to law.

LAW AND JUSTICE

The total disregard of the ethical implications of the law tends to reduce analytical jurisprudence to a system rather arid formation.

IN ENGLAND

Two different words, "Law" and "Justice" are a constant reminder that these are two different things and not the same thing. And their use tends to hide from viewing the real and intimate relation which exists between them.

AND IN CONTINENT

(Rechet : Right = Droit : Law)
Continental speech conceals the difference between 'law' and 'ri[illegible]ereas English speech conceals the connection between the[illegible]

Law:—

"We term any kind of rule or canon whereby actions are framed a law". [Hooker]

"Law in its most general sense signifies a rule of action, and is indiscriminately to all kinds of action whether rational or irrational, animate or inanimate. Thus we say, the Laws of motion, of gravitation, of optics, of nature and of nations". [Blackstone]

Kinds of Laws:—

1. Imperative Law
2. Physical Law or Scientific Law
3. Natural or Moral Law
4. Conventional Law
5. Customary Law
6. Practical or Technical Law
7. International Law
8. Civil Law or the Law of the State.

LAW

"We term any kind of rule or canon, whereby actions are framed as law."

[*Hooker*]

"Law in its most general sense signifies a rule of action, and is indiscriminate to all kinds of action whether rational or irrational, animate or inanimate."

Thus, we say, the Laws of motion, of gravitation, of optics, of nature and of nations."

{Blackstone}

KINDS OF LAWS

(1) Imperative Law

(2) Physical Law or Scientific Law

(3) Natural or Moral Law

(4) Conventional Law

(5) Customary Law

(6) Practical or Technical Law

(7) International Law

(8) Civil Law or the Law of the State

108

1. Imperative Law means a rule of action imposed upon men by some authority which enforces obedience to it.

'A Law is a command which obliges a person or persons to a course of ~~action~~ conduct.' {Austin}

The sanction of imperative Law - Punishment, Law etc.

Positive morality in society also amounts to the Imperative Laws.

Hobbes' view:— [It is men and arms that make the force and power of the laws. (Hobbes).]

2. Physical Law is an expression of actions as they are. (moral Law or the law of reason, is an expression of actions as they ought to be.)

3. Natural or Moral Law means the principles of natural right and wrong — the principles of natural justice including all rightful actions.

Justice being of two kinds the Positive and Natural.

Natural justice is justice as it is indeed and in truth.

Positive justice is justice as it is conceived, recognized and expressed.

(1) Imperative Law means a rule of action imposed upon men by some authority which enforces obedience to it. 'A Law is a command which obliges a person or persons to a course of conduct'.

The sanction of Imperative Law – punishment, wars, etc.

{Austin}

Positive morality in society also amounts to Imperative Laws.

Hobbes Views : It is men and arms that make the force and power of the Laws.

(Hobbes)

(2) Physical Law is an expression of actions as they are. (Moral Law or the Law of Reason is an expression of actions as they ought to be).

(3) Natural or Moral Law means the principles of natural right and wrong — the principles of natural justice including rightful actions.

Justice being of two kinds — the Positive and Natural.

Natural justice is justice as it is indeed and in truth.

Positive justice is justice as it is conceived, recognised and expressed.

4. Conventional Law:— is any rule or system of rules agreed upon by persons for the regulation of their conduct. Agreement is a law for the parties to it.

5. Customary Law:— is any rule of action which is actually observed by men — any rule which is the expression of some actual uniformity of voluntary action. Custom is law for those who observe it.

6. Practical or Technical Law— consists of rules for the attainment of some practical end. e.g. games there are both conventional laws and Practical laws: the former being the rules agreed upon by players, the latter being the rules to make the player successful or for the successful playing of the game.

7. International Law:— consists of those rules which govern sovereign states in their relations and conduct towards each other.

1, Express laws. [Treaties Etc.
2, Implied laws. [Customary.

Again divisible into two kinds—

1, Common laws (between all nations)
2, Particular laws (between two or more particular nations.)

8. Civil Law:— Law of the State or of the land, as applied in the Courts of Justice.

(4) Conventional Law is any rule or system of rules agreed upon by persons for the regulation of their conduct. Agreement is a law for the parties to it.

(5) Customary Law is any rule of action which is actually observed by men — any rule which is the expression of some actual uniformity of voluntary action. Custom is law of those who observe it.

(6) Practical or Technical Law consists of rules for the attainment of some practical end. In games, there are both 'Conventional Laws' and 'Practical Law', the former being the rules agreed upon by players, the latter being the rules to make the play a success or for the successful playing of the game.

(7) International Law consists of those rules which govern sovereign states in their relations and conduct towards each other.

(1) Express Laws (Treaties, etc.)

(2) Implied Laws (Customary)

Again divisible into two kinds:

(3) Common Laws (between all nations)

(4) Particular Laws (between two or more particular nations)

(8) Civil Law: Law of the State or of the land; as applied in the courts of justice.

110

Punishment:—

Political Crimes:—

We agree with the great body of legislators in thinking, that though, in general a person who has been a party to a criminal design, which has not been carried into effect,* yet an exception to this rule must be made with respect to high offences against the State; for State Crimes, and especially the most heinous and formidable State crimes, have this peculiarity, that, if they are successfully committed, the criminal is almost always secure from punishment. The murderer is in greater danger after his victim is despatched than before. The thief is in greater danger after the purse is taken than before. But the rebel is out of danger as soon as he has subverted the Govt. As the penal law is impotent against a successful rebel, it is consequently necessary that it should be made strong and sharp against the first beginning of rebellion..."

* [be not ~~dealt with~~ severely dealt with]

[I L.C.C. Judgement 1916]
PP 120.

PUNISHMENT

POLITICAL CRIMES

We agree with the great body of legislators in thinking that though, in general, a person who has been a party to a criminal design, which has not been carried into effect be not severely dealt with, yet an exception to this rule must be made with respect to high offences against the State; for State crimes, and especially the most heinous and formidable State crimes, have this peculiarity, that, if they are successfully committed, the criminal is almost always secure from punishment. The murderer is in greater danger after his victim is despatched than before. The thief is in greater danger after the purse is taken than before; but the rebel is out of danger as soon as he has subverted the Government. As the penal law is impotent against a successful rebel, it is consequently necessary that it should be made strong and sharp against the first beginning of rebellion..."

[II L.C.C. judgement, 1916

pp. 120]

Punishment :—

Dream that merited Capital punishment } :— When Marsyas dreamed that he had cut Dionysius' throat, the tyrant put him to death, arguing that he would have never dreamt of such a thing by night, had he not thought of it by day.

—————— : o : ——————

Capital punishment and Draco's Law } :— The Laws of Draco affixed the penalty of death to almost all crimes alike, to petty thefts, for instance, as well as, to sacrilege and murder; and the only explanation Draco is said to have given of that is, that minor offences deserve that penalty and he could find no greater for more heinous.

—————— : o : ——————

Punishment – is thought by many philosophers to be a necessary evil.

—————— : o : ——————

State and man } The State is not really an end in itself and man is not here for the sake of Law or the State but that these rather exist for ~~the~~ man.

—————— : o : ——————

PUNISHMENT

Dream the merited Capital Punishment

When Marsyas dreamed that he had cut Dionysius throat, the tyrant put him to death, arguing that he would have never dreamt of such a thing by night, had he not thought of it by day.

———————: * :———————

CAPITAL PUNISHMENT AND DRACO'S LAW

The Laws of Draco affixed the penalty of death in almost all crimes alike, to petty thefts, for instance, as well as to sacrilege and murder; and the only explanation Draco is said to have given of that is, that minor offences deserve that penalty, and he could find no greater for more heinous.

Punishment is thought by many philosophers to be a necessary evil.

———————: * :———————

STATE AND MAN

The State is not really an end in itself and man is not here for the sake of Law or the State, but that these rather exist for man.

———————: * :———————

112

Justice :— The maintenance of right within a political community by means of the physical force of the State.
It has replace the personal vengeance, when men avenged their own wrongs by themselves or with the help of their kinsmen. In those days the principle of 'might is right' worked.

II. Civil & Criminal Justice } :— Civil justice enforces rights. Criminal justice punishes wrongs.

A man claims a debt that is due to him, or the restoration of property wrongfully detained from him. This is Civil.
In a Criminal case the defendant is accused of a wrong. Court visits the accused with a penalty for the duty already disregarded and for a right already violated, as where he is hanged for murder and imprisoned for theft.

JUSTICE

The maintenance of right within a political community by means of the physical force of the State.

It has replaced the personal vengeance, when men avenged their own wrongs by themselves or with the help of their kinsmen. In those days, the principle of 'Might is Right' worked.

CIVIL AND CRIMINAL JUSTICE

Civil Justice enforces rights. Criminal justice punishes wrongs.

A man claims a debt that is due to him, or the restoration of property wrongfully detained from him. This is Civil.

In a Criminal Case, the defendant is accused of a wrong. Court visits the accused with a penalty for the duty already disregarded and for a right already violated, as where he is hanged for murder and imprisoned for theft.

Both in Civil and Criminal ~~law~~ proceedings, there is a wrong complained of.

In civil it amounts to a claim of right;
In Criminal it amounts merely to an accusation of wrong.
Civil justice is concerned primarily with the plaintiff and his rights;
Criminal with defendant and his offence.

The Purposes of Criminal Justice

Punishment:—

There this can not be useful in cases of disinterested 'offenders' such as politicals. It can't be an evil bargain for him.

1. Deterrent:— Chief end of the law is to make the evildoer an example and a warning to all that are like-minded with him. It makes every offence, an ill bargain to the offender. (Changing motive)

2. Preventive:— In the second place it is preventive or disabling. Its special purpose is to prevent a repetition of wrongdoing by the disablement of the offender.

Justification of Capital punishment

We hang murderers, not merely that it may deter others, but for the same reason for which we kill snakes, namely because it is better for us that they should be out of the world than in it.

3. Reformative:— Offences are committed through the influence of motives upon character, and may be prevented either by a change of motives or by a change of character. Deterrent punishment acts in the former method while Reformative deals with the second.

Jail Diary-113

Both in civil and original proceedings, there is a *wrong* complained of.
In Civil it amounts to a claim of right.
In Criminal, it amounts nearly to an accusation of wrong.
Civil justice is concerned primarily with the plaintiff and his rights.
Criminal with defendant and his offence.

———————— : * : ————————

THE PURPOSES OF CRIMINAL JUSTICE PUNISHMENT

1. Deterrent: Chief end of the Law is to make the evil-doer an example and a warning to all that are like-minded with him. It makes every offence "an ill bargain to the offender"* (Changing motive).

2. Preventive: In the second place, it is preventive or disabling. Its special purpose is to prevent a repetition of wrong doing by the disablement of the offender.

JUSTIFICATION OF CAPITAL PUNISHMENT

We hang murderers not merely that it may deter others, but for the same reason for which we kill snakes, namely because it is better for us that they should be out of the world than in it.

3. Reformative: Offences are committed through the influence of motives upon characters, and may be prevented either by a change of motives or by a change of character.

Deterrent punishment acts in the former event while Reformative deals with

* Then this cannot be useful in cases of disinterested 'offenders', such as politicals. It can be an evil bargin for him. – Bhagat Singh

114

'Advocates of 'Reformative theory' admit only such forms of penalty as are subservient to the education and discipline of the criminal, and reject all those which profitable only as deterrent or disabling. Death is in their view no fitting penalty; 'we must cure our criminals not kill them.' Flogging and other corporal punishments are condemned as relics of barbarism. Such penalties are considered by them to be degrading and brutalising both to those who suffer and to those who inflict them.

Result of severe punishment. Dangerous & desperate class of criminals springs up.

The more ~~coercive~~ efficient the action of the State, the more successful it is in restraining all normal human beings from the dangerous paths, and the higher becomes the proportion of degeneracy among those who break the law.

4. Retributive Punishment:—

'It gratifies the instinct of revenge or retaliation, which exists, not merely in the individual wronged, but also by way of sympathetic extension in the society at large.

According to this view, it is right and proper, that evil should be returned for evil. An eye for an eye and a tooth for a tooth is deemed a plain and selfsufficient rule of natural justice. Punishment becomes an end in itself.

The most horrible theory! People thinking in these terms are really maintaining the barbaric penalties of ancient and pre-civilization times.

Advocates of 'Reformative theory' admit only such forms of penalty as are subservient to the education and discipline of the criminal, and reject all those which (are) profitable only as deterrent or disabling. Death is in their view no fitting penalty; 'we must cure our criminals, not kill them.' Flogging and other corporal punishments are condemned as relics of barbarism. Such penalties are considered by them to be degrading and brutalising both to those who suffer and to those who inflict them.*

The more efficient the coercive action of the State, the more successful it is in restraining all normal human beings from the dangerous paths, and the higher becomes the proportion of degeneracy among those who break the law.

4. Retributive Punishment

It gratifies the instinct of revenge or retailiation, which exists not merely in the individual wronged, but also by way of sympathetic extension in the society at large.

According to this view, it is right and proper that evil should be returned for evil. An eye for an eye and a tooth is deemed a plain and self-sufficient rule of natural justice. Punishment becomes an end in itself.**

---

* Result of severe punishment: Dangerous and desperate class of criminal springs up. – Bhagat Singh's comment.

** The most horrible theory! People thinking in these terms are really maintaining the barbaric practices of ancient and pre-civilisation times. – Bhagat Singh's comment.

Punishment an evil:— Punishment is in itself an evil, and can be justified only as the means of attaining a greater good

But the — Supporters of Retributive theory argue this way:— "Guilt plus punishment is equal to innocence."

"The wrong whereby he has transgressed the law of right, has incurred a debt. Justice requires that the debt be paid. ∴ The first object of punishment is to satisfy the outraged Law."

Peine forte et dure was death with torture.. ∴ Judgement for which was delivered as follows:—

"That you be taken back to the prison whence you came, to a long dungeon into which no light can enter; that you be laid on your back on the bare floor, with a cloth round your loins, but elsewhere naked; that there be set upon your body a weight of iron as great as you can bear, and greater; that you have no substance save, on the first day, three morsels of the coarsest bread; on the second day, three draughts of stagnant water from the pool nearest to the prison door; on the third day again three morsels of bread as before and such bread and such water alternately from day to day untill you die."

This punishment was inflicted on people of both the sexes alike for all sorts of offence not extraordinary.

PUNISHMENT AN EVIL

Punishment is in itself an evil, and can be justified only as the means of attaining a greater good.

But the supporters of retributive theory argue this way: "Guilt plus punishment is equal to innocence."

"The wrong whereby he has transgressed the law of tight, has incurred a debt. Justice requires that the debt be paid... The first object of punishment is to satisfy the outraged law."

: * :

Peine forte et dure was death with torture... judgement for which was delivered as follows:

"That you be taken back to the prison whence you came, to a long dungeon into which no light can enter; then you be laid on your back on the bare floor, with a cloth round your loins, but elsewhere naked, that there be set upon your body a weight of iron as great as you can bear, and greater; that you have no substance save, on the first day, the morsels of the coarsest bread; on the second day, three draughts of stagnant water from the pool nearest to the prison door; on the third day, again three morsels of bread as before, and such bread and such water alternately from day to day until you die."*

* This punishment was inflicted on people of both the sexes alike for all sorts of offence, not for extraordinary. – Bhagat Singh.

116

Foreign Subjection :—

Subjection to foreign yoke is one of the most potent causes of the decay of nations. —— Prof: E. A. Ross.

Domination of a democracy over foreign nations :— No rule over a foreign people is so exacting and so merciless in its operations as that of a democracy. Lalaji

Marriage

Dr. Tagore holds that the marriage system all over the world — and not only in India — from the earliest ages till now, is a barrier in the way of the true union of man and woman, which is possible only when society shall be able to offer a large field for the creative work of woman's special faculty, without detracting the creative work in the home.

FOREIGN SUBJECTION

Subjection to foreign yoke is one of the most potent causes of the decay of nations.

— Prof. A.E. Ross

DOMINATION OF A DEMOCRACY AND FOREIGN NATIONS

No rule over a foreign people is so exacting and so merciless in its operations as that of a democracy.

— Lalaji

MARRIAGE

Dr. Tagore holds that the marriage system all over the world — and not only in India — from the earliest ages till now is a barrier in the way of the true union of man and woman, which is possible only when society shall be able to offer a large field for the creative work of woman's special faculty, without detracting the creative work in the home.

: * :

117

Citizen & Man

The Spartan Pedaretes presented himself for admission to the council of the Three Hundred and was rejected; he went away rejoicing that there were 300 Spartans better than himself. I suppose he was in earnest, there is no reason to doubt it.

That was a citizen.

A Spartan mother had five sons with the army. A Helot arrived; trembling she asked his news. "Your five sons are slain." "Vile slave, was that what I asked thee?" "We have won the victory." She hastened to the temple to render thanks to the gods.

That was a citizen.

Emile' PP 8

: o :

Life & Education:—

People think only of preserving their child's life; this is not enough, he must be taught to preserve his own life when he is a man, to bear the buffets of fortune, to brave wealth and poverty, to live at need among the snows of Iceland or on the scorching rocks of Malta. In vain you guard against death; he must needs die; and even if you do not kill him with your precautions, they are mistaken.

Teach him to live rather than to avoid death: life is not breath, but action, the use of our senses, our mind, our faculties, every part of ourselves which makes us conscious of our being. Life consists less in length of days than in keen sense of living. A man may be buried at a hundred and may never have lived at all. He would have fared better had he died young.

Emile' PP 10

: o :

CITIZEN AND MAN

The Spartan Pedaretes presented himself for admission to the Council of the Three Hundred and was rejected; he went away rejoicing that there were 300 Spartans better than himself. I suppose he was in earnest; there is no reason to doubt it.

That was Citizen.

A Spartan mother had five sons with the army. A Helot arrived; trembling, she asked his news. "Your five sons are slain."

"Vile slave, was that what I asked thee?"

"We have won the victory." She hastened to the temple to render thanks to the gods.

That was a citizen.

—————————— : * : ——————————

LIFE AND EDUCATION

People think only of preserving their child's life; this is not enough, he must be taught to preserve his own life when he is a man, to bear the buffets of fortune, to brave wealth and poverty, to live at need among the snows of Iceland or on the scorching rocks of Malta. In vain you guard against death; he must need die; and even if you do not kill him with your precautions, they are mistaken.

Teach him to live rather than to avoid death! Life is not breath, but action! The use of our senses, our mind, our faculties, every part of ourselves which makes us conscious of our being. *Life consists less in length of days than in keen sense of living*. A man may be buried at a hundred and may never have lived at all. He would have fared better had he died young.

—————————— : * : ——————————

118

Truth:— Truth however does not ~~lead~~ lead to fortune, and the people confer neither embassies, nor professorships, nor pensions.

Rousseau 122
S.C.

Crime and Criminals

"... with readymade opinions one cannot judge of crime. Its philosophy is a little more complicated than people think. It is acknowledged that neither convict prisons, nor the hulks, nor any system of hard labour ever cured a criminal. These forms of chastisement only punish him and reassure society against the offences he might commit. Confinement, regulation, and excessive work have no effect but to develop with these men profound hatred, a thirst for forbidden enjoyment and frightful recalcitrations. On the other hand I am convinced that the celebrated cellular system gives results which are specious and deceitful. It deprives a criminal of his force, of his energy, enervates his soul by weakening and frightening it, at last exhibits a dried up mummy as a model of repentance and amendment."

The House of the Dead PP 17
Dostoevsky

TRUTH

Truth however does not lead to fortune, and the people confer neither embassies, nor professorships, nor pensions.

Rousseau. S.C.

——————— : * : ———————

CRIME AND CRIMINALS

"...With readymade opinions one cannot judge of crime. Its philosophy is a little more complicated than people think. It is acknowledged that neither convicted prisoners, nor the hulks, nor any system of hard labour ever cured a criminal. These forms of chastisement only punish him and reassure society against the offences he might commit. Confinement, regulation, and excessive work have no effect but to develop with these men profound hartred, a thirst for forbidden enjoyment and frightful recalcitrations. On the other hand, I am convinced that the celebrated cellular system gives results, which are specious and deceitful. It deprives a criminal of his force, of his energy, enervates his soul by weakening and frightening it, at last exhibits a dried up memory as a model of repentance and amendment."

The House of the Dead

Fyodor Dostoevsky

119

Desire vs Contentment!

A conscious being whose powers were equal to his desires would be perfectly happy. .... The mere limitation of our desires is not enough, for if they were less than our powers, part of our faculties would be idle, and we should not enjoy our whole being; neither is the mere extension of our powers enough, for if our desires were also increased we should only be the more miserable. True happiness consists in decreasing the difference between our desires and our powers.

44. Emile

DESIRE VS. CONTENTMENT!

A conscious being whose powers were equal to his desires would be perfectly happy . . . The mere limitation of our desires is not enough, for if they were less than our powers, part of our faculties would be idle, and we should not enjoy our whole being, neither is the mere extension of our power enough, for if our desires were also increased, we should only be the more miserable. True happiness consists in decreasing the difference between our desires and our powers.

— Emile

120

Bourgeois revolution is germinated by the circumstance already existing in its predecessor regime.

" The bourgeois revolution usually ends with the seizure of power. For the proletarian revolution the seizure of power is only a ~~begg~~ beginning; power, when seized, is used as a lever for the transformation of the old economy and for the organization of a new one." P. 20.

" There still remain two gigantic and extremely difficult tasks—(even after the overthrow of the existing regime in one country—say Russia).

First of all comes the internal organization

The second crucial problem is that of the world revolution ...; the need to solve international problems, the need to promote the world revolution—(without which communist regime can not be quite safe from the international capitalist threat.) P. 21. 22

"Bourgeois revolution is germinated by the circumstance already existing in its predecessor regime."

"The bourgeois revolution usually ends with the seizure of power. For the protetarian revolution, the seizure of power is only a beginning; power, when seized, is used as a level for the transformation of the old economy and for the organisation of a new one."

"There still remain two gigantic and extremely difficult tasks — (even after the overthrow of the existing regime in one country — say Russia)."

First of all comes the internal organisation.

The second crucial problem is that of the world revolution . . . The need to solve international problems, the need to promote the world revolution (without which Communist regime cannot be quite safe from the international capitalist threat.)

I. If the proletariat is to win over the majority of the population, it must first of all overthrow the bourgeoisie and seize the powers of the State.

II. Next, it must establish the Soviet authority breaking up the old State apparatus, and thus at one blow counteracting the influence which the bourgeoisie and the petty bourgeois apostles of class collaboration exercise over the working (though non-proletariat) masses.

III. Thirdly, the proletariat must completely and finally destroy the influence which the bourgeoisie and petty bourgeois compromisers exercise over the majority of the working (though non-proletarian) masses, it must do so by the revolutionary satisfaction of the economic needs of these masses at the cost of the exploiters.

Nicolai Lenin
P. 23

Dictatorship of the proletariat means the masses guided and directed by the Communist Party. Though party exercise substantial influence or control, still it is not all. Apart from its guidance, the 'will' of the masses is necessary for the achievement of any particular object.

"We have to admit that the broad masses of the workers must be led and guided by the class-conscious minority." and that is the Party. Party has 'Trade unions' to link the Party with proletariat (labour), 'Soviets' to link it with all the labouring masses in the political field, 'Co-operatives' in the economic field especially

I. If the proletariat is to win over the majority of the population, it must first of all overthrow the bourgeoisie and seize the powers of the State.

II. Next, it must establish the Soviet authority breaking up the old State apparatus, and, thus, at one blow counteracting the influence which the bourgeoisie and the petty-bourgeiosie apostles of class collaboration exercise over the working (though non-proletariat) masses.

III. Thirdly, the proletariat must completely and finally destroy the influence which the bourgeoisie and petty-bourgeois compromisers exercise over the majority of the working (though non-proletarian) masses; it must do so by the revolutionary satisfaction of the economic needs of these masses at the cost of the exploiters.

— Nikolai Lenin

———————— : * : ————————

Dictatorship of the proletariat means the masses guided and directed by the Communist Party. Though party exercises substantial influence or control, still it is not all. Apart from its guidance, the 'will' of the masses is necessary for the achievement of any particular object.

"We have to admit that the broad masses of the workers must be led and guided by the class-conscious minority. And that is the Party." Party has 'Trade Unions' to link the Party with proletariat labour, 'Soviets' to link it with all the labouring masses in the political field, 'Cooperative' in the economic field, especially to

(contd.)

122

to link the peasantry, 'League of youth' to train communists from amongst the rising generation. Finally Party itself is the sole guiding force with-in the Dictator-ship of the proletariat.

link the peasantry, 'League of Youth' to train Communists from amongst the rising generation. Finally, Party itself is the sole guiding force within the dictatorship of the proletariat.

Figures: —

Inequality of incomes: —

Production

Pre-war United Kingdom's (England's) Annual production amounted to: —

£, 2000,000,000

Gained through foreign investments: —

£, 200,000,000

Total £ 2200,000,000

Distribution

$\frac{1}{9}$ of the whole population i.e. Capitalist or bourgeois took away $\frac{1}{2}$ of the total production i.e. — £, 1100,000,000. [least average income annual — £ 160]

$\frac{2}{9}$ th of the whole population i.e. Petty bourgeois took away $\frac{1}{3}$ of the remaining half or $\frac{1}{6}$ th of the whole — i.e. £, 300,000,000. {average income less than £ 160 a year}

$\frac{2}{3}$ rd of the population i.e. manual labour or proletariat got the rest i.e. £, 800,000,000. [average income £ 80 yearly]

United States America: — in 1890.

40% of total production was received by owners of means

60% " was given to all workers.

FIGURES

INEQUALITY OF INCOMES

Production

Pre-war United Kingdom's (England's) Annual production amounted to	: £ 2000.000,000
Gained through foreign investments	: £ 200.000,000
Total	£ 2200,000,000

Distribution

1/9th of the whole population, i.e. capitalist or bourgeois took away 1/2 of the total production i.e. £ 1100,000,000	least average income annual £ 160
2/9th of the whole population i.e. petty bourgeois took away 1/3 of the remaining half or 1/6th of the whole, i.e. 300.000,000	average income less than 160 a year
2/3rd of the population i.e. manual labour or proletariat got the rest, i.e. 800,000,000	average income £ 60 yearly

: * :

UNITED STATES OF AMERICA: IN 1890

4% of total production was received by the owners of means.

60% of total production was given to all workers.

124

Aim of Life: —

" The aim of life is nomore to control mind, but to develope it harmoniously, not to achieve salvation hereafter, but to make the best use of it here below, and not to realize truth, beauty and good only in contemplation, but also in the actual experience of daily life; social progress depends not upon the ennoblement of the few but on the enrichment of the many; and spiritual democracy or universal brotherhood can be achieved only when there is an equality of opportunity in the social, political and industrial life."

AIM OF LIFE

"The aim of life is no more to control mind, but to develop it harmoniously; not to achieve salvation hereafter, but to make the best use of it here below, and not to realise truth, beauty and good only in contemplation, but also in the actual experience of daily life; social progress depends not upon the ennoblement of the few but on the enrichment of the many; and spiritual democracy or universal brotherhood can be achieved only when there is an equality of opportunity in the social, political and industrial life."

———————— : * : ————————

* 125 to 164 are blank

Science of the State !!

Ancient Polity :— Rome & Sparta :— Aristotle & Plato :—

Subordination of the individual to the State was the dominant feature of these ancient polities, Sparta & Rome. In Hellas or in Rome the citizen had but a few personal rights; his conduct was largely subject to public censorship, and his religion was imposed by State authority. The only true citizens and members of the Sovereign body being an aristocratic caste of freemen, whose manual work is performed by slaves possessing no civil rights.

<u>Socrates</u> :— Socrates is represented as contending that whoever, after reaching man's estate, voluntarily remains in a city, should submit to the Govt. even when he deems its laws unjust; accordingly, on the ground that he would break his covenant with the State by escaping from prison, he determines to await the execution of his sentence.

Plato :— [Social Contract] He traces the origin of society and the State to mutual need, for men as isolated beings are incapable of satisfying their manifold wants. He, while depicting a kind of idealised Sparta, says, "In an ideal State philosophers should rule; and to this aristocracy or government of the best, the body of citizens would owe implicit obedience." He emphasises on the careful training and education of citizens.

Aristotle :— He was the first to disentangle politics from ethics, though he careful not to sever them. "The majority of men," he urged, "are ruled by their passions rather than by reason, and the State must therefore train them to virtue by a life-long course of discipline, as in Sparta. Until political society is instituted there is no administration of justice . . . (but) it is necessary to enquire into the best constitution

SCIENCE OF THE STATE

Ancient Polity: Rome and Sparta: Aristotle and Plato

Subordination of the individual to the State was the dominant feature of these ancient polities, Sparta and Rome. In Hellas or in Rome, the citizen had but a few personal rights: his conduct was largely subject to public censorship, and his religion was imposed by State authority. The only true citizens and members of the sovereign body being an aristocratic caste of freedom, whose manual work is performed by slaves possessing no civil rights.

: * :

SOCRATES

Socrates is represented as contending that whoever, after reaching man's estate, voluntarily remains in a city, should submit to the Government, even when he deems its laws unjust; accordingly, on the ground that he would break his *covenant* with the State by escaping from prison into exile, he determines to await the execution of an unjust sentence.

: * :

PLATO

(Social Contract)

He traces the origin of society and the State to mutual need, for men as isolated beings are incapable of satisfying their manifold wants. He, while depicting a kind of idealised Sparta, says, "In an ideal State, philosophers should rule; and to this aristocracy or government of the best, the body of citizens would owe implicit obedience." He emphasises on the careful training and education of citizens.

: * :

ARISTOTLE

He was the first to disentangle politics from ethics, though he was careful not to sever them. "The majority of men," he argued, "are ruled by their passions rather than by reason, and the State must, therefore, train them to rule by a life-long course of discipline, as in Sparta. Until political society is instituted, there is no administration of justice... (but) it is necessary to enquire into the best constitution and best system of legislation."

(contd.)

and the best system of legislation.

"The germ of the State is found in the family or household. From the union of many households arose the village community, ... members being subject to patriarchal government.

"By the association of several villages was formed the State, a natural, independent, and self-sufficing organization.

"But while the household is ruled monarchically, in constitutional governments the subjects are free and on an equality with their rulers.

"Natural sociability and mutual advantage impel men to union. Man is by nature a political (social) animal.

"The State is much more than an alliance which individuals can join or leave without effect, for the independent or cityless man is unscrupulous and savage, something essentially different from a citizen."

Plato:— Plato had anticipated this conception of the State as a body whose members combine harmoniously for a common end.

Aristotle:— Aristotle held that where freedom and equality prevail there should be alternate rule and subjection, but it is best, if possible, that the same persons should always rule.

In opposition to Plato's communism, he argued in favour of duly regulated private property, considering that only a moral unity is possible or desirable in the State.

[illegible] He divided governments into monarchies, aristocracies, and republics and their respective perversions, tyrannies, oligarchies and democracies, according as the supreme power is in the hands of one or a few or the many, and according as the aim is the general good or the private interests of the rulers, regard also being paid to freedom, wealth, culture and nobility.

Each polity consists of three parts — the deliberative, the executive, and the judicial bodies. Citizenship is constituted neither by residence, nor by the possession of legal rights, but by participation in judicial power and Public office.

The many, having attained a certain standard of morality, should rule; for, though individually inferior, they are collectively wiser and more virtuous than a select few. But, while undertaking all deliberative and judicial functions, they should be excluded from the highest executive offices.

The best Polity is that in which the middle class between the very rich and the very poor controls the government, for that class has most permanent life, and is the most·

"The germ of the State is found in the family or household. From the union of many households arose the village community... members being subject to patriarchal government.

"But while the household is ruled monarchically, in constitutional governments, the subjects are free and on equality with their rulers.

"Natural sociability and mutual advantage implements union. Man is by nature a political (social) animal.

"The State is much more than an alliance which individuals can join or leave without effect, for the independent or cityless man is unscrupulous and savage, something different from a citizen."

PLATO

Plato had anticipated this conception of the State as a body whose members combine harmoniously for a common end.

ARISTOTLE

Aristotle held that where freedom and equality prevail, there should be alternate rule and subjection, but it is best, if possible, that the same persons should always rule.

In opposition to Plato's Communism, he argued in favour of duly regulated private property, considering that only a moral unity is possible or desirable in the State.

KINDS OF GOVERNMENTS

He divided governments into monarchies, aristocracies, and republics and their respective perversions, tyrannies, oligarchies and democracies, according as the supreme power is in the hands of one or a few or the many, and according as the end is the general good or the private interests of the rulers, regard also being paid to freedom, wealth, culture and nobility.

Each polity consists of three parts: (1) the deliberative, (2) the executive, and (3) the judicial bodies. Citizenship is constituted neither by residence, nor by the possession of legal rights, but by participation in judicial power and public office.

The many, having attained a certain standard of morality, should rule, for though individually inferior, they are collectively wiser and more virtuous than a select few. But, while undertaking all deliberative and judicial functions, they should be excluded from the highest executive offices. The best polity is that in which the middle class between the very rich and the very poor controls the government, for that class has most permanent life and is the most.

conformable to reason, as well as the most capable of constitutional action. This is virtually an affirmation that sovereignty should reside in the majority of the citizens, slaves of course being ignored.

Democracies agree in being based on equality in respect of personal liberty, which implies the eligibility of all citizens to hold, or elect to the offices of State, and the rule of each over all and of all over each in turn.

Aristotle, like Plato, treated democracy as a debased form of Govt, and held that it is more suitable to large states than any others.

Stoics :—

Cynics :—

Epicureans :— "Justice" said Epicurus, is nothing in itself, but merely a compact (as the basis of justice) of expediency to prevent mutual injury.

Stoic :— A disciple of the philosopher Zeno (340–260 B.C.) who opened (ōm) his school in a colonnade called the "Stoa Poikilē" [painted porch] at Athens. Later Roman stoics were Cato the Younger, Seneca, Marcus ~~and~~ Aurelius. The word Stoic literally means, 'one indifferent to pleasure or pain.'

Stoicism is a school of philosophy strongly opposed to Epicureanism in its view of life and duty; ~~strongly~~ indifferent to pleasure or pain.

Cynicism :— A sect of philosophers founded by Antisthenes of Athens (born c. 444 B.C.) characterised by an ostentatious contempt for riches, arts, science and amusements. They are called Cynics because of their morose manners. Cynicism is sometimes used to denote the ~~[illegible]~~ contempt for human nature.

Epicureans :— Epicurus [341–270 B.C.] was a Greek Philosopher, who taught that pleasure was the chief good. Epicureans is used to denote one devoted to luxuries of the table or given to sensual enjoyment.

conformable to reason, as well as the most capable of constitutional action. This is virtually an affirmation that sovereignty should reside in the majority of the citizen, slaves of course being ignored.

Democracies agree in being based on equality in respect of personal liberty, which implies the eligibility of all citizens to hold, or elect to the offices of State, and the rule of each over all and of all over each in turn.

Aristotle, like Plato, treated democracy as a debased form of Government and held that it is more suitable to large states than any others.

STOICS

CYNICS

EPICUREANS

"Justice," said Epicurus "is nothing in itself, but merely a compact (as the basis of justice) of expediency to prevent mutual injury."

STOIC(ISM)

A disciple of the philosopher Zeno (340-360 B.C.) who opened his school in a colonnade called the 'Stoa Poikite' (painted porch) at Athens. Later, Roman stoics were Cato the Younger, Seneca. Marcus Aurelius. The word Stoic literally means, 'one indifferent to pleasure or pain'. Stoicism is a school of ancient philosophy strongly opposed to Epicureanism in its view of life and duty.

CYNICISM

A sect of philosophers founded by Antisthenes of Athens (born c. 444 B.C.) characterised by an ostentatious contempt for riches, arts, science and amusements. They are called Cynics because of their morose manners. Cynicism is sometimes used to denote the contempt for human nature.

EPICUREANS

Epicurus (341-270 B.C.) was a Greek Philosopher, who taught that pleasure was the chief good. Epicurean is used to denote one devoted to luxuries of the table or given to sensual enjoyment.

168

Roman Polity:— 'Little of direct importance was added to political theory by the Romans but in a closely allied department viz; jurisprudence—they made contributions of deep interest and value.'

Jus Civile / *Jus Gentium*

Under the Republic there had grown up beside the "Civil Law" (*Jus Civile*) a collection of rules and principles called *Jus Gentium* (Law of nations) which represented the common features prevailing among the Italian tribes.

Jus Naturale

The great Roman *jurisconsults* (experts in the science of Law) [deriving the idea from the Stoics] came gradually to identify the Law of Nature [*Jus Naturale*] with the *Jus Gentium*.

They taught that this Law was divine and eternal, and that it was superior in majesty and validity to the laws of particular States. Natural Law was supposed to be actually existent and bound up with Civil Law.

In the *Antonian Era*, when Roman Law attained a high development and Stoic doctrines were most influential, the jurists formulated as juridicial but not as political principles the maxims that

'All men were born free'

and that by the Law of nature, 'All men are equal'— the implication being that although the civil law recognized class distinction all mankind were equal before the Law of Nature.

Social Contract in Roman Politics

Though the Roman jurists did not postulate a contract as the origin of Civil Society, but there is a tendency to deduce recognised rights and obligations from a supposed, but non-existent contract.

With regard to sovereignty, the citizens assembled in the *Comitia tributa* exercised the supreme power during the golden days of the Republic.

Under the Empire, the sovereign authority was vested in the Emperor, and according to the later jurisconsults, the people, by the *Lex Regia*, delegated the supreme command to each Emperor at the beginning of his reign, thus conferring on him all their rights to govern and legislate.

ROMAN POLITY

'Little of direct importance was added to political theory by the Romans, but in a closely allied department, viz jurisprudence — they made contributions of deep interest and value.'

JUST-CIVIK JUST-GENTIUM

Under the Republic, there had grown up, beside the 'Civil Law' (Just-Civik), a collection of rules and principles called Jus Gentium (Law of Nations) which represented the common features prevailing among the Italian tribes.

JUS NATURALE

The great Roman juris-consults (experts in the Science of Law) [deriving the idea from the Stoics] came gradually to identify the Law of Nature (Jus Naturale) with the Jus Gentium.

They taught that this Law was divine and eternal, and that it was superior in majesty and validity to the laws of particular States. Natural Law was supposed to be actually existent and bound up with Civil Law.

In the *Antonian Era*, when Roman Law attained a high development and Stoic doctrines were most influential, the jurists formulated as juridical but not as political principles the maxims that: "all men were born free" and that, by the Law of Nature, "all men are equal," the implication being that although the Civil Law recognised class distinction, all mankind were equal before the Law of Nature.

SOCIAL CONTRACT IN ROMAN POLITY

Though the Roman jurists did not postulate a contract as the origin of Civil Society, there is a tendency to deduce recognised rights and obligations from a supposed, but non-existent contract.

With regard to sovereignty, the citizens assembled in the Comitia Tributa exercised the supreme power during the golden days of the Republic.

Under the Empire, the sovereign authority was vested in the Emperor, and according to the later juris consults, the people, by the Lex Regia, delegated the supreme command to each Emperor at the beginning of his reign, thus conferring on him all their rights to govern and legislate.

Middle Ages:-

Thomas Aquinas

Thomas Aquinas:- [1226–1274] is said to be the chief representative of the middle ages political theory. He following Roman jurists, recognized a *natural law*, the principles of which have been divinely implanted in human reason, together with *positive laws* that vary in different States.

He held that the legislative power, the essential attribute of sovereignty should be directed to the common good, and that, for the attainment of this end, it should *belong to the multitude* or *to their representative*, the prince. A mixed government of *monarch*, *nobles*, and *people* with *the Pope* as final authority, seemed to him the best.

Marsilius of Padua:— [Dies 1328]

In his 'Defensor Pacis', Marsilius of Padua advocates the doctrine of *popular sovereignty*, and *combated the papal pretensions to temporal power* that had been based on the False Decretals.

[Idea of contract]

Since *men adopted civil life for their mutual advantage*, the laws ought to be made by the body of citizens; for laws are not likely to be the best possible, nor to be readily obeyed, unless enacted by those whose interests are directly affected and who know what they need.

[Sovereignty of the people]

He affirmed that the *legislative power belonged to the people*, and that the legislature should institute the executive, which it may change or depose.

Renaissance — Reformation!!

In renaissance, all departments of knowledge were vitalized and the circumscribed philosophy — having served as a handmaid of theology for a thousand years, rapidly gave place to a new philosophy of *nature and man*, more liberal, more profound, and more comprehensive.

Bacon recalled man from metaphysics to nature and actuality.

Philosophy must begin with universal scepticism. But one fact is soon found to be indubitable: the existence of a thinking principle in man. *The existence of Consciousness!*

[Cartesian Philosophy]

The appeal to subjective conviction, to the authority of the individual, which was so strongly emphasized in the Reformation, thus becomes the very basis of *Cartesian Philosophy*.

Cartesian = Relating to a French Philosopher René Descartes [1596–1650 A.D.] and his Philosophy.

MIDDLE AGES

Thomas Aquinas

Thomas Aquinas (1226-1274) is said to be the chief representative of the middle age political theory. He, following Roman jurists, recognised a natural law, the principles of which have been divinely implanted in human reason, together with positive laws that vary in different States. He held that the legislative power, the essential attribute of sovereignty, should be directed to the common good, and that, for the attainment of this end, it should belong to the multitude or to their representative, the prince. A mixed government of monarch, nobles, and people, with the Pope as final authority, seemed to him the best.

MARSILIO OF PADUA*

Idea of Contract

In his' *Defensor Pacis'*, Marsilio of Padua advocated the doctrine of popular Sovereignty, and combated the Papal pretensions to temporal power that had been based on the False Decretals.

SOVEREIGNTY OF THE PEOPLE

Since men adopted civil life for their mutual advantage, the laws ought to be made by the body of citizens; for laws are not likely to be the best possible, nor to be readily obeyed, unless enacted by those whose interests are directly affected and who know what they need.

He affirmed that the legislative power belongs to the people, and that the legislature should institute the executive, which it may also change or depose.

RENAISSANCE-REFORMATION!!

In Renaissance, all departments of knowledge were vitalised and the circumscribed philosophy – having served as a hand-maid of theology for a thousand years, rapidly gave place to a new philosophy of Nature and Man, more liberal, more profound, and more comprehensive. Bacon recalled man from metaphysics to nature and actuality.

Philosophy must begin with universal scepticism. But one fact is soon found to be indubitable: the existence of a thinking principle in man. The existence of consciousness!

CARTESIAN PHILOSOPHY

The appeal to subjective conviction, to the authority of the individual, which was so strongly emphasised in the Reformation, thus becomes the very basis of Cartesian Philosophy.

Cartesian = Relating to a French philosopher Rene Descartes (1596-1650 A.D.) and his philosophy.

* Died in 1328. – Bhagat Singh

170

New Period:— After Reformation the Papal authority having been shaken off a wave of freedom swept [minds of] both the rulers and the people. But there was confusion. To settle new situation great many thinkers began to meet all over the question of State. Different schools grew up.

Machiavelli:— Machiavelli — the famous Italian political thinker thought the Republican form of Govt. to be the best one, but ~~fearing~~ doubting the stability of such a form of Govt. he inculcated maxims of securing a strong princely rule and hence he wrote '*The Prince*'

His advocacy of centralized Govt. had greatly affected political theory and practice in Europe.

Machiavelli was perhaps the first writer who treated 'Politics' from a purely secular point of view.

Other Thinkers:— [Pact & Contract] Majority of other favoured the theory of pact or contract. [In Roman Law a pact ~~or con~~ was the product of an agreement among individuals, and fell short of a contract, which was a pact plus an obligation]

There were two different sects of these thinkers. The first one expounded the theory based on the Hebrew idea of covenant between God and man supplemented by the Roman idea of contract. It postulated a tacit contract between the government and the people.

The second or modern form, relates to the institution of political society by means of a compact among individuals. Prominent thinkers of this school were Hooker, Hobbes, Locke and Rousseau.

Defenders of Popular liberty:— [Huguenot]

1. The Vindiciae contra Tyrannos (1579), ascribed to Huguenot Languet, contended that kings derive their power from the people's will, and that if a king violates the compact to observe the laws which he and the people promise conjointly at the institution of royalty, the latter are absolved from allegiance.

[Buchanan]

2. Buchanan also held that the king and people are mutually bound by a pact, and that its violation by the former entails forfeiture of his rights.

NEW PERIOD

After Reformation, the Papal authority having been shaken off, a wave of freedom swept the minds of both the rulers and the people. But there was confusion. To settle the new situation, great many thinkers began to meditate over the question of State. Different schools grew up.

MACHIAVELLI

Machiavelli, the famous Italian political thinker, thought the Republican form of Government to be the best one, but doubting the stability of such a form of government, he inculcated maxims of securing a strong princely rule and hence he wrote *The Prince*. His advocacy of centralised government had greatly affected political theory and practice in Europe.

Machiavelli was perhaps the first writer who treated 'politics' from a purely secular point of view.

OTHER THINKERS

[Pact and Contract]

Majority of others favoured the theory of pact or contract. {In Roman Law, a pact was the product of an agreement among individuals and fell short of a contract, which was a pact plus an obligation].

There were two different sects of these thinkers. The first one expounded the theory based on the Hebrew idea of covenant between God and man supplemented by the Roman idea of contract. It postulated a tacit contract between the government and the people.

The second or modern form relates to the institution of Political Society by means of a contract among individuals. Prominent thinkers of the school were Hooker, Hobbes, Locke and Rousseau.

DEFENDERS OF POPULAR LIBERTY

Huguenot

(1) The Vindiciae Contra Tyrannos (1579), ascribed to Huguenot Languets, contended that kings derive their power from the people's will, and that if a king violates the contract to observe the laws which he and the people promise conjointly at the institution of royalty, the latter are absolved from allegiance.

[BUCHANAN]

(2) Buchanan also held that the king and people are mutually bound by a pact, and that its violation by the former entails forfeiture of his rights.

171

Jesuits:— Even the Jesuits Bellarmine and Mariana argued that kings derived their authority from the people, but they are subject to Pope—

[King James I] (1609) James I admitted this theory in a speech to Parliament in 1609, saying that "every just king in a settled kingdom is bound to observe that paction made to his people by his laws, in framing his government agreeable thereunto."

[Convention Parliament] 1688 Convention Parliament declared in 1688 that James II, "having endeavoured to subvert the constitution by breaking the original contract between the king and people," had rendered the throne vacant.

Bodin:- 1586 'The first comprehensive political philosopher of modern times', Bodin, author of the 'Republic' [1577 and 1586] says that 'force and not a contract is the origin of a commonwealth.' Primitive patriarchal governments were overthrown by conquest, and natural liberty was thus lost.

In his opinion "Sovereignty was the supreme power over citizens. He regarded 'sovereignty' as independent, indivisible, perpetual, inalienable, and absolute power. He confused his idea of sovereignty with the then existing kingship.

Althusius:— [1557–1638] He is notable for clearly asserting that sovereignty resides in the people alone, kings being only their magistrates or administrators, and that the sovereign rights of the community are inalienable.

Grotius:— [1625] In his work, 'De Jure Belli et Pacis' [1625], Grotius holds that man has a strong desire for a peaceable and ordered society. But he inculcates the theory of non-resistance and denies that the people are always and everywhere sovereign, or that all government is established for the sake of the governed. Sovereignty arises either from conquest or from consent; but he lays emphasis on the idea that sovereignty, the indivisible power

Hooker:— He in his ~~Ecclesi~~ "Ecclesiastical Polity" Book I [1592–3] postulates an original state of nature in which all men were equal and subject to no law. Desire for a life suitable to man's dignity and aversion to solitude, impelled them to unite in 'politic societies'. 'Natural inclination' and an order expressly or secretly agreed upon touching the manner of their union in living together, were the two foundations of the present 'politic societies', the latter that we call 'the laws of a commonweal'.

JESUITS

(3) Even the Jesuits Bellarmine and Mariana agrued that kings derived their authority from the people, but they are subject to Pope.

[KING JAMES I 1609]

James I admitted this theory in a speech to Parliament in 1609, saying that "every just king in a settled kingdom is bound to observe that pact made to his people by his laws, in framing his government agreeable there unto."

[CONVENTION PARLIAMENT 1588]

Convention Parliament declared in 1688 that James II, "having endeavoured to subvert the constitution by breaking the original contract between the king and people," had rendered the throne vacant.

BODIN [1586]

'The first comprehensive political philosopher of modern times, Bodin, author of the *Republic* [1577 and 1586] says that "force and not a contract is the origin of a commonwealth". Primitive patriarchal governments were overthrown by conquest and natural liberty was thus lost.

In his opinion "Sovereignty was the supreme power over citizens." He regarded "sovereignty as independent indivisible, perpetual, inalienable and absolute power. He confused his idea of sovereignty with the then existing kingship.

ALTHUSIUS [1557-1638]

He is notable for clearly asserting that sovereignty resides in the people alone, kings being only their magistrates or administrators; and that the sovereign rights of the community are inalienable.

GROTIUS [1625]

In his work, De Jure belli et Paris (1628), Grotius holds that man has a strong desire for a peaceful and ordered society. But he inculcates the theory of non-resistance and denies that the people are always and everywhere sovereign, or that all government is established for the sake of the governed. Sovereignty arises either from conquest or from consent; but he lays emphasis on the idea that sovereign is the indivisible power.

HOOKER

He, in his Ecclesiastical Polity, Book 1 (1529-30) postulates an original state of nature in which all men were equal and subject to no Law. Desire for a life suitable to man's dignity, and aversion to solitude, impelled them to unite in 'politic societies'. 'Natural inclination' and an order expressly or secretly agreed upon touching the manner of their union in living together, were the two foundations of the present 'politic societies'. It is the latter that we call "the Laws of a Commonweath".

172

[Origin of State]

Sovereignty or Legislative power controls the Executive as well

"Sovereignty of the people" :–

"To take away all mutual grievances, injuries and wrongs, the only way was to ordain some kind of government, or common judge:
He admits with Aristotle that the origin of government was in Kingship.
But he says, 'Laws not only teach what is good, but also have a constraining force, derived from the consent of the governed, expressed either personally or through representatives.'

> "Laws human of what kind soever, are available [i.e. valid] by consent."
> "Laws they are not which public approbation hath not made so."

Thus he clearly affirms that sovereignty or legislative power, resides ultimately in the people.

1620 :– Famous declaration of the "Pilgrim Fathers" on board the 'Mayflower' (1620), "We do solemnly and mutually in the Presence of God and of one another covenant and combine ourselves together into a civil Body Politic."

1641 :– The Agreement of the People of England (another famous Puritan document, which emanated from the army of the Parliament) [1647] also indicates the same tendency of mind.

Milton :– In his 'Tenure of kings and magistrates' (1649) he also propounds similar principles. He affirms that "all men naturally were borne free," they "agreed by common league to bind each other from mutual injury and jointly to defend themselves against any that gave disturbance or opposition to such agreement. Hence came towns, cities and commonwealths." "This authority and power of self-defence and preservation being originally and naturally in every one of them and unitedly in all, was vested in kings and magistrates as deputies and commissioners."

(1649)

Sovereignty of the People

> The Power of kings and magistrates is nothing else but what is only derivative, transferred, and committed to them in trust from the people to the Common good of all, in whom the power yet remain fundamentally and cannot be taken from them without a violation of their natural birth-right. Hence nations may choose or depose kings, merely by the right and liberty of freeborn men to be governed as seems them best.

ORIGIN OF STATE

Sovereignty: Legislative Power controlling the Executive as well

'To take away all mutual grievance, injuries and wrongs, the only way was to ordain some kind of government, or common judge'. He admitted with Aristotle that the origin of government was in kingship. But he says, 'Laws not only teach what is good, but also have a constraining force, derived from the consent of the governed, expressed either personally or through reprsentatives'.

"Laws, human of what kind so ever, are available {i.e. valid} by consent."

"Laws they are not which public approbation hath not made so."

SOVEREIGNTY OF THE PEOPLE

Thus he clearly affirmed that sovereignty or legislative power resides ultimately in the people.

1620

Famous Declaration of the "Pilgrim Fathers" on board the Mayflower (1620): "We do solemnly and mutually in the presence of God and of one another convenant and combine ourselves together into a Civil Body Politic.

1647

Agree to the People of England: (Another famous Puritan document, which emanated from the Army of the Parliament) (1647) also indicates the same tendency of mind.

MILTON

1649 [Sovereignty of the People]

In his *Tenure of Kings and Magistrates* (1649), he also propounds similar principles. He affirms that "all men naturally were born free". They "agreed by common league to bind each other from mutual injury and jointly to defend themselves against any that gave disturbance or opposition to such agreement. Hence came towns, cities and commonwealths!" "This authority and power of self-defence and preservation being originally and naturally in everyone of them and unitedly in all, was vested in kings and magistrates as deputies and commissioners!

The Power of kings and magistrates is nothing else but what is only derivative, transferred, and committed to them in trust from the people to the common good of all, in whom the power yet remains fundamentally and cannot be taken from them without a violation of their natural birth-right. Hence, nations may choose or depose kings, merely by the right and liberty of freeborn men to be governed as seems them best.

<u>Theory of Divine Rights of Kings</u>:— In this very age when great many thinkers were thus propounding these principles of "sovereignty of the people" there were other theorists, who tried to prove that kingdoms being enlarged families, the patriarchal authority of the head of a household was transferred by primogenitary descent to "the representative of the first sovereign who could be proved to have reigned over any nation. <u>Monarchy was therefore presumed to rest on an indefeasible right</u>, and the king was held responsible <u>to God alone</u>! This was known as "<u>Divine Rights of kings</u>!" This was known as the "<u>Patriarchal Theory</u>"!

[Patriarchal Theory!]

<u>Thomas Hobbes</u>:— In his various works written in 1642 – 1650 – 1651 he combined the doctrine of the unlimited authority of the sovereign, with the rival doctrine of an original compact of the people. Hobbes's defence of absolutism — passive obedience — was secular and rationalistic rather than theological. He regarded the happiness of the community (as a whole) as the great end of government.

Hobbes' philosophy is cynical. According to him a man's impulses are naturally directed to his own preservation and pleasure and he can not aim at anything but their gratification. <u>Therefore man is unsociable by nature</u>! He says "In the natural state <u>every man is at war with his fellows</u>, and the life of every one is in danger, solitary, poor, nasty, brutish and short." It is the <u>fear of this solitary life that impel them to political union</u>. Since mere pact would not do, hence the establishment of "<u>a supreme common power</u>" "the Govt."

[man an unsociable Animal!]

[Perpetual danger forces them to form State!]

Society is founded by "<u>acquisition</u>" i.e. by conquest, or "<u>institution</u>" viz; by mutual contract or compact. In the latter case, once the sovereign authority is established all must obey. Anybody rebelling must perish. He should be destroyed.

{"Conquest" or "acquisition" and "Institution" the only basis of State}

He gives the rights of legislature, judicature and Executive — one and all to the Sovereign. "To be effective", he writes, "the sovereign power must be unlimited, irreclaimable and indivisible. Unlimited power may indeed give rise to mischiefs but the worst of these is not so bad as Civil war or anarchy.

{Unlimited Authority of the Sovereign!}

THEORY OF DIVINE RIGHTS OF KINGS

Patriarchal Theory

In this very age when great many thinkers were thus propounding these principles of 'sovereignty of the People', there were other theorists, who tried to prove that kingdom(s) being enlarged families, the patriarchal authority of the head of a household was transferred by primogenitary descent to the representative of the first sovereign who could be proved to have reigned over any nation. Monarchy was, therefore, presumed to rest on an indefensible right and the king was held responsible to God alone! This was konwn as "Divine Rights of Kings!" This was known as the "Patriarchal Theory!"

THOMAS HOBBES

In his various works written in 1642-1650-1651, he combined the doctrine of the unlimited authority of the sovereign with the rival doctrine of an original compact of the people. Hobbes' defence of absolutism — passive obedience — was secular and rationalistic rather than theological. He regarded the happiness of the community (as a whole) as the great end of government.

Man an Unsociable Animal: Perpetual Danger Forces them to Form State.

Hobbes' philosophy is cynical. According to him, a man's impulses are naturally directed to his own preservation and pleasure, and he cannot aim at anything but their gratification. Therefore, man is unsociable by nature! He says, "In the natural stage, every man is at war with his fellows; and the life of everyone is in danger, solitary, poor, unsafe, brutish and short." It is the fear of this sort of life that impels them to political union. Since mere pact wouldn't do, hence, the establishment of a supreme common power' – the Government."

"Conquest" or "Acquisition" and "Institution" the only Basis of all States.

Society is founded by "acquisition", i.e., by conquest, or "institution", viz. by mutual contract or compact. In the latter case, once the sovereign authority is established, all must obey. Anybody rebelling must perish. He should be destroyed.

Unlimited authority of the Sovereign!

He gives the rights of Legislature, Judicature and Executive — one and all to the Sovereign. "To be effective," he writes, – "the sovereign power must be unlimited, irreclaimable and indivisible. Unlimited power may indeed give rise to mischief, but the worst of these is not so bad as civil war or anarchy."

In his opinion, monarchy, aristocracy or democracy do not differ in their power. Their achievement towards general peace and security rests on the obedience of the public or people they command. Anyhow he prefers 'Monarchy'! 'Limited monarchy' is the best in his opinion. But he professes that the sovereign must regulate ~~[illegible]~~ ecclesiastical as well as civil affairs, and determine what doctrines are conducive to peace.

Thus he holds a clear and valid doctrine of sovereignty, while retaining the fiction of a social contract to generate the king or sovereign.

Spinoza:— [1677] [unsociability of man!]

[In his work Tractatus Politicus, 1677] regarded man as originally having equal rights over all things; hence the state of nature was a State of War. Men, led by their reasons freely combined their forces to establish Civil Government. As man had absolute power, hence the Sovereign authority thus established had the absolute power. In his opinion 'Right' and 'Power' are identical. Hence the sovereign being vested with the 'power' had all the 'rights' ipso facto. Hence he favours 'absolutism'.

Pufendorf:— [Law of Nature and of Nations 1672]. In his opinion man is a sociable animal, naturally inclined towards family and peaceful life.

Experience of injuries that one man can inflict on another leads up to Civil Government, which is constituted (1) by a unanimous mutual covenant of a number of men to institute a commonwealth, (2) by the resolution of the majority that certain rulers shall be placed in authority (3) by a covenant between the Govt and the subjects that the former shall rule and the latter shall obey lawful commands!

In his opinion, monarchy, aristocracy or democracy do not differ in their power. Their achievement towards general peace and security rests on the obedience of the public or people they command. Anyhow he prefers 'Monarchy'! 'Limited Monarchy' is the best in his opinion. But he presses that the sovereign must regulate ecclesiastical as well as civil affairs, and, determine what doctrines are conducive to peace.

Thus, he holds a clear and valid doctrine of sovereignty, while retaining the fiction of a social contract to generate the king or sovereign.

SPINOZA [1677]

Unsociability of Men

[In his work, *Tractatus Politicus*, 1677] regarded men as originally having equal rights over all things; hence, the state of nature was a State of War. Men, led by their reasons freely combined their forces to establish Civil Government. As men had absolute power, hence the sovereign authority thus established had the absolute power. In his opinion, 'Right' and 'Power' are identical. Hence, the Sovereign being vested with the 'power' had all the 'rights' ipso-facto. Hence, he favours 'absolutism'.

PUFFENDOR

[*Law of Nature and of Nations*, 1672] In his opinion, man is a sociable animal, naturally inclined towards family and peaceful life.

Experience of injuries that one man can inflict on another leads up to civil Government, which is constituted (1) by a unanimous mutual convenant of number of men to institute a Commonwealth, (2) by the resolution of the majority that certain ruler shall be placed in authority, (3) by a covenant between the Governments and their subjects that the former shall rule and the latter shall obey lawful commands!

Locke — [Two Treatises of Civil Government- 1690]

'No man has a natural right to govern.'

He portrays the state of nature — a state of freedom and equality in respect of jurisdiction and dominion, limited only by natural law or reason, which prohibits men from harming one another in life, health, liberty and possessions, the punishment requisite by way of restraint or reparation being in everyman's hands.

State of Nature! 'Men living together according to reason without a common superior on earth with authority to judge between them is properly the State of Nature!'

Private Property! 'Everyman has a natural right of property in his own person and in the product of his own labour exercised on the materials of nature. As much land as a man tills, plants, improves, cultivates, and can use the product of, so much is his property.'

Property & Civil Society! According to him "property" is antecedent to "Civil Society"!

Origin of Civil Society! But it appears men were in some sort of dangers and fears, and therefore they renounced their natural liberty in favour of civil liberty. In short, necessity, convenience, and inclination urged men into society.

Definition of Civil Society! Those who are united into one body and have a common established law and judicature to appeal to, with authority to decide controversies between them and punish offenders are in "Civil Society."

Consent:- Conquest is not an 'original' of government. Consent was and could be the sole origin of any lawful government.

The legislative assembly is not absolutely arbitrary over the lives, liberties and property of the people, for it possesses only the joint power which the separate members had prior to the formation of the society, and which they resigned to it for particular and limited purposes.

Law:- 'The end of Law is not to abolish or restrain but to preserve or enlarge freedom.'

Legislative:- The legislative being only a fiduciary power for certain ends the people may remove or alter it when it violates the trust reposed in it.

Ultimate sovereignty of the People! Thus the community always retains the supreme power or ultimate sovereignty, but does not assume it until the government is dissolved.

LOCKE

[Two Treatises of Civil Government, 1690]

"No man has a natural right to govern."

He portrays the state of nature — a state of freedom and equality in respect of jurisdiction and dominion, limited only by natural law or reason, which prohibits men from harming one another in life, health, liberty and possessions, the punishment requisite by way of restraint or reparation being in every man's hands.

STATE OF NATURE!

"Men living together according to reason without a common superior on earth with authority to judge between them is properly the State of Nature!"

PRIVATE PROPERTY!

"Every man has a natural right of property in his own person and in the product of his own labour exercised on the material of nature. As much land as a man tills, plants, improves, cultivates, and can use the product of, so much is his property."

PROPERTY AND CIVIL SOCIETY!

According to him, "property" is antecedent to "civil society"!

ORIGIN OF CIVIL SOCIETY!

But it appears men were in some sort of dangers and fears, and, therefore, they renounced their natural liberty in favour of civil liberty. In short, necessity, convenience, and inclination urged men into society.

DEFINITION OF CIVIL SOCIETY!

Those who are united into one body, and have a common established Law and judicature to appeal to, with authority to decide controversies between them and punish offenders, are in a civil society.

CONSENT

Conquest is not an origin of government. Consent was, and could be, the sole origin of any lawful government.

The legislative assembly is not absolutely arbitrary over the lives, liberties and property of the people, for it possesses only the joint power which the separate members had prior to the formation of the society, and which they resigned to it for particular and limited purposes.

LAW

"The end of Law is not to abolish or restrain but to preserve or enlarge freedom."

LEGISLATIVE

The legislative being only a fiduciary power for certain ends, the people may remove or alter it, when it violates the trust reposed in it.

ULTIMATE SOVEREIGNTY OF THE PEOPLE!

Thus, the community always retains the supreme power or ultimate sovereignty, but does not assume it until the government is dissolved.

176

Legislative & Executive

To prevent the sacrifice of the general welfare to private interests, it is expedient that the legislative and executive powers should be in different hands, the latter being subordinate to the former.

Where both powers are vested in an absolute monarch there is no civil government, for there is no common judge with authority between him and his subjects.

The forms of different commonwealths in free societies are Democracy, oligarchy, or elective monarchies together with mixed forms.

"Right of Revolution"! — "A Revolution is justifiable when the government ceases to fulfil its part of contract — the protection of personal rights."

Rousseau

Rousseau.

Equality. — No one should be rich enough to buy another nor poor enough to be forced to sell himself. Great inequalities pave the way for tyranny.

Property & Civil Society. — The first man who, having enclosed a piece of land, thought of saying 'this is mine,' and found people simple enough to believe him, was the true founder of Civil Society.

What wars, crimes, and horrors would have been spared to the race if some one had exposed this imposture, and declared that the earth belonged to no one, its fruits to all.

LEGISLATIVE AND EXECUTIVE

To prevent the sacrifice of the general welfare to private interests, it is expedient that the legislative and executive powers should be in different hands, latter being subordinate to the former.

Where both powers are vested in an absolute monarch, there is no civil government, for there is no common judge with authority between him and his subjects.

The forms of different commonwealths in free society are Democracy, Oligarchy, or elective Monarchies together with mixed forms.

: * :

RIGHT OF REVOLUTION!

"A Revolution is justifiable when the government ceases to fulfil its part of contract — the protection of personal rights."

Rousseau

ROUSSEAU

EQUALITY*8

No one should be rich enough to buy another nor poor enough to be forced to sell himself. Great inequalities pave the way for tyranny.

: * :

PROPERTY AND CIVIL SOCIETY

The first man who, having enclosed a piece of land, thought of saying 'that is mine', and found people simple enough to believe him, was the true founder of Civil Society.

What wars, crimes, and horrors would have been spared to the race, if some one had exposed this imposture, and declared that the earth belonged to no one, and its fruits to all.

* This and other quotes are from Rousseau's social contract.

"The man who meditates is a depraved animal"

Civil Law

Pointing to the oppression of the weak and the insecurity of all, the rich craftily devised rules of justice and peace, by which all should be guaranteed their possessions, and established a supreme ruler to enforce the laws.

This must have been the origin of society and of the laws, which gave new chains to the weak and new strength to the rich, finally destroyed natural liberty, and, for the profit of a few ambitious men, fixed for ever the law of property and of inequality, converted a clever usurpation into an irrevocable right and subjected the whole human race hence-forward to labour, servitude and misery.

Re: inequalities

But it is manifestly opposed to natural law that a handful of people should gorge superfluities while the famished multitude lack the necessaries of life

"The man who meditates is a depraved animal."

———————— : * : ————————

CIVIL LAW

Pointing to the oppression of the weak and the insecurity of all, the rich craftily devised rules of justice and peace, by which all should be guaranteed their possessions, and established a Supreme ruler to enforce the laws.

This must have been the origin of society and of the laws, which gave new chains to the weak and new strength to the rich, finally destroyed natural liberty and, for the profit of a few ambitious men, fixed for ever the law of property and if inequality, converted a clever usurpation into an irrevocable right, and subjected the whole human race henceforward to labour, servitude and misery.

———————— : * : ————————

RE : INEQUALITIES

But it is manifestly opposed to natural law that a handful of people should gorge superfluities while the famished multitude lack the necessities of life.

178

Fate of his writings | Emile & Social Contract, both published in 1762, the former burnt in paris, Rousseau narrowly escaping arrest, the both being publically burnt in Genoa, his native place whence he expected greater response.

Sovereignty of monarchs to that of the people | Rousseau retains the French ideas of unity and centralisation; but while in the Seventeenth Century the State (or sovereignty) was confounded with the monarchy, Rousseau's influence caused it in the 18th Century to be identified with the people.

Pact | By pact men exchange natural liberty for civil liberty and moral liberty.

: o :

Right of first occupancy | Right of property:—

Its justification depends on these conditions: (a) that the land is uninhabited; (b) that a man occupies only the area required for his subsistence, (c) that he takes possession of it not by an empty ceremonial, but by labour and cultivation.

FATE OF HIS WRITINGS

Emile and social contract, both published in 1762, the former burnt in Paris, Rousseau narrowly escaping arrest, then both being publically burnt in Geneva, his native place whence he expected greater response.[9]

SOVEREIGNTY OF MONARCH TO THAT OF PEOPLE

Rousseau retains the French ideas of unity and centralisation, but while in the seventeenth century, the State (or sovereignty) was confounded with the monarchy, Rousseau's influence caused it in the 18th century to be identified with the people.*

PACT

By pact men exchange natural liberty for civil liberty and moral liberty.

: * :

RIGHT OF FIRST OCCUPANCY

Its justification depends on these conditions: (a) that the land is uninhabited; (b) that a man occupies only the area required for his subsistence; (c) that he takes possession of it not by an empty ceremonial, but by labour and cultivation.

* Bhagat Singh's comments.

Religion :— { Rousseau places even religion under the tyranny of the sovereign.

Introductory Note.—

I wish to enquire whether, taking men as they are and laws as they can be made, it is possible to establish some just and certain rule of administration in civil affairs...

.. I shall be asked whether I am a prince or a legislator that I write on politics. I reply that I am not. If I were one, I should not waste time in saying what ought to be done, I should do it or remain silent

: o :

Man is born free, and everywhere he is in chains.

: o :

Shaking off the yoke of slavery by force!

I should say that so long as a people is compelled to obey and does obey, it does well; but that, so soon as it can shake off the yoke and does shake it off, it does better; for, if men recover their freedom by virtue of the same right (i.e. force) by which it was taken away, either they are justified in resuming it or there was no justification for depriving them of it.

RELIGION

Rousseau places even religion under the tyranny of the sovereign.[10]

INTRODUCTORY NOTE

I wish to enquire whether, taking men as they are and laws as they can be made, it is possible to establish some just and certain rule of administration in civil affairs...

"....I shall be asked whether I am a prince or a legislator that I write on politics. I reply that I am not. If I were one, I should not waste time in saying what ought to be done, I should do it or remain silent."

: * :

Man is born free and everywhere he is in chains.

: * :

SHAKING OFF THE YOKE OF SLAVERY BY FORCE!

I should say that so long as a people is compelled to obey and does obey, it does well; but that, so soon as it can shake off the yoke and does shake it off, it does better; for, if men recover their freedom by virtue of the same right (i.e. force) by which it was taken away, either they are justified in resuming it, or there was no justification for depriving them of it.

* Bhagat Singh's comments.

Force

"Power which is acquired by violence is only a usurpation, and lasts only so long as the force of him who commands prevails over that of those who obey; so that if the latter become the strongest in their turn and shake off the yoke, they do so with as much right and justice as the other who had imposed it on them. The same law (of force) which has made the authority then unmakes it; it is the law of the strongest."

Diderot. Encyclopaedia "Authority."

Slaves lose everything in their bonds, even the desire to escape from them!

The Right of the Strongest

"Obey the powers that be. If that means, Yield to force, the precept is good but superfluous; I reply that it will never be violated.

Right of slavery

"Do subjects, then, give up their persons on condition that their property also shall be taken? I do not see what is left for them?"

"It will be said that the despot secures to his subjects civil peace. Be it so; but what do they gain by that,

FORCE

"Power which is acquired by violence is only a usurpation, and lasts only so long as the force of him who commands prevails over that of those who obey, so that if the latter become the strongest in their turn and shake off the yoke, they do so with as much right and justice as the other who had imposed it on them. The same law (of force) which has made the authority, then unmakes it, is the law of the strongest."

Diderot, Encyclopaedia

"Authority"

Slaves lose everything in their bonds, even the desire to escape from them.

: * :

RIGHT OF THE STRONGEST

"Obey the powers that be. If that means, yield to force, the precept is good but superfluous; I reply that it will never be violated."

: * :

RIGHT OF SLAVERY

"Do subjects, then, give up their persons on condition that their property also shall be taken? I do not see what is left for them?"

"It will be said that the despot secures to his subjects civil peace. Be it so, but what do they gain by that,

(contd.)

of the wars which his ambitions brings upon them, together with his insatiable greed and the vexations of his administration, harass them more than their own dissensions would?

To say that a man gives himself for nothing is to say what is absurd and inconceivable".

Whether addressed by a man to a man, or by a man to a nation, such a speech as this will always be equally foolish: "I make an agreement with you wholly at your expense and wholly for my benefit, and I shall observe it as long as I please, while you also shall observe it as long as I please."

Equality:

If then you wish to give stability to the State, bring the two extremes as near together as possible; tolerate neither rich nor beggars. These two conditions, naturally inseparable, are equally fatal to the general welfare; from the one class spring tyrants, from the other, the supporters of tyranny; it is always between these that the traffic in public liberty is carried on; the one buys the other sells.

---

if the wars which his ambitions bring upon them, together with his insatiable greed and the vexations of his administration, harass them more than their own dissensions would.

"To say that a man gives himself for nothing is to say what is absurd and inconceivable."

Whether addressed by a man to a man, or by man to a nation, such a speech as this will always be equally foolish: "I make an agreement with you wholly at your expense and wholly for my benefit, and I shall observe it as long I please while you also shall observe it as long as I please.

: * :

EQUALITY

If then you wish to give stability to the State, bring the two extremes as near together as possible; tolerate neither rich nor beggars. These two conditions naturally inseparable are equally fatal to the general welfare; from the one class spring tyrants, from the other, the supporters of tyranny; it is always between these that the traffic in public liberty is carried on; the one buys and the other sells.

: * :

182

Hail lays waste a few cantons, but it rarely causes scarcity. Riots and civil wars greatly startle the chief men; but they do not produce the real misfortunes of nations, which may be abated, while it is being disputed who shall tyrannize over them. It is from their permanent conditions that their real prosperity or calamities spring; when all is left crushed under the yoke, it is then that everything perishes; it is then that the chief men, destroying them at their leisure, "Where they make a solitude, they call it peace." "P.P. 176"

"Hail lays waste a few cantons, but it rarely causes scarcity. Riots and civil wars greatly startle the chief men, but they do not produce the real misfortunes of nations, which may be abated, while it is being disputed who shall tyrannise over them. It is from their permanent conditions that their real prosperity or calamities spring; when all is left crushed under the yoke, it is then that everything perishes; it is then that the chief men, destroying them at their leisure, "where they make a solitude, they call it peace."

———————— : * : ————————

French Revolution:—

America | American war of Independence had great effect on the French situation. (1776)

Taxes | Court or ministry acting under the use of the name, 'The King', framed the edicts of taxes at their own discretion and sent them to the Parliament to be registered; for until they were registered by the Parliament they were not operative.

The court insisted that the Parliament's authority went no farther than to show reasons against it, reserving to itself the right of determining whether the reasons were well or ill founded and in consequence thereof, either to withdraw the edict as a matter of choice, or to order it to be enregistered as a matter of authority.

The Parliament on the other hand insisted for having the right of rejection.

M. Calonne the minister wanted money. He was aware of the sturdy disposition of the Parliament with respect to taxes. He called an "Assembly of Notables" (1787).

It was not a States-General which was elected but all the members were nominated by the King and consisted of 140 members. Even then he could not get the majority support. He divided it into 7 committees. Every committee consisting of 20 members. Every question was to be decided by majority votes in committees and by majority committee votes in Assembly. He tried to have 11 members whom he could trust in each of any four committees, thus to have a majority. But his devices failed

FRENCH REVOLUTION

America

American War of Independence had great effect on the French situation (1776).

Taxes

Court or ministry, acting under the use of the name 'The King', framed the edicts of taxes at their own discretion and sent them to Parliament to be registered; for until they were registered by the Parliament, they were not operative.

The court insisted that the Parliament's authority went no further than to show reasons against it, reserving to itself the right of determining whether the reasons were well or ill founded and, in consequence therefore, either to withdraw the edict as a matter of choice, or to order it to be unregistered as a matter of authority.

The Parliament, on the other hand, insisted for having the right of rejection.

M. Calonne, the minister, wanted money. He was aware of the sturdy disposition of the Parliament with respect to taxes. He called an "Assembly of Notables" (1787).

It was not a States-General which was elected, but all the members were nominated by the King and consisted of 141 members. Even then he could not have the majority support. He divided it into 7 committees. Every committee consisted of 20 members. Every question was to be decided by majority votes in committees and by majority committee votes in Assembly. He tried to have 11 members whom he could trust in each or/any four committees, thus to have a majority. But his devices failed.

184

M. de Lafayette was vice president of a second committee. He charged ~~with~~ M. Calonne for having sold crown land to the amount of two millions of livres. He gave it in writing too. Sometimes afterwards M. Calonne was dismissed.

The Archbishop of Tolouse was appointed the Prime Minister and Finance Minister. He placed before the Parliament two Taxes — Stamp Tax and a sort of land-tax. The Parliament returned for answer,

> That with such a revenue as the nation then supported the name of taxes ought not to be mentioned but for the purpose of reducing them,

and threw both the edicts out. Then they were ordered to Versailles, where the king held 'a Bed of justice' and enregistered those edicts. Parliament returned to Paris, Held a session there. Ordered the enregistration to be struck off. Declaring everything done at Versailles to be illegal. All were served with letter de cachets and exiled. And afterwards they were recalled, Again the same edicts were placed before them.

M. De Lafayatte was vice president of a second committee. He charged M. Calonne for having sold crown land to the amount of two millions of lives. He gave it in writing too. Sometimes afterwards, M. Calonne was dismissed.

The Archbishop of Tolouse was appointed the Prime Minister and Finance Minister. He placed before the Parliament two taxes — Stamp Tax and a sort of land-tax. The Parliament returned for answer.

That with such a revenue as the nation then supported, the name of taxes ought not to be mentioned but for the purpose of reducing them, and threw both the edicts out. Then they were ordered to Versailles, where the King held 'A Bed of Justice' and unregistered those edicts. Parliament returned to Paris. Held a session there. Ordered the unregistration to be struck off, declaring everything done at Versailles to be illegal. All were served with 'letter de cachets and exiled'. And afterwards they were recalled. Again the same edicts were placed before them.

Then arose the question of calling a States-general The King promised with the Parliament. But ministery opposed. They put forth a new proposal for the formation of a 'Full Court'. It was opposed on two grounds. Firstly for principles' sake govt had no right to change itself. Such a precedent will be harmful. Secondly on the question of forms it was contended that it was nothing but an enlarged Cabinet.

The Parliament rejected this proposal. It was beseiged by armed forces. For many days they were there. Still they persisted. Then many of them were arrested and sent to different jails.

A deputation from Brittany came to remonstrate against it. They were sent to Bastille.

"Assembly of notables" again recalled, decided to follow the same course as adopted in 1614 to call States General.

"Parliament decided that 1200 members should be elected, 600 from Commons, 300 from Clergy and 300 from Nobility.

States General ~~had~~ met in May 1789. Nobility and Clergy went to two different Chambers

Then arose the question of calling a States General. The king promised with the Parliament. But ministry opposed. They put forth a new proposal for the formation of a 'Full Court'. It was opposed on two grounds: Firstly, for principle's sake, Government had no right to change itself. Such a precedent will be harmful. Secondly, on the question of form, it was contended that it was nothing but an enlarged Cabinet.

The Parliament rejected this proposal. It was beseiged by armed forces. For many days, they were there. Still they persisted. Then many of them were arrested and sent to different jails.

A deputation from Brittany came to remonstrate against it. They were sent to Bastille.

"Assembly of Notables" again recalled, decided to follow the same course as adopted in 1614 and call States General.

"Parliament decided that 1200 members should be elected, 600 from commons, 300 from clergy and 300 from nobility."

<u>States General</u> met in <u>May 1789</u>. Nobility and Clergy went to two different chambers.

186

The third estate or the Commons refused to recognize this right of the clergy and nobility and declared themselves to be the 'Representatives of the Nation' denying the others any right whatsoever in any other capacity than the national representatives sitting along with them in the same chamber. Hence the States General became the 'National Assembly.' They sent invitations to other chamber. Majority of clergy came over to them. 45 of the Aristocracy also joined them, then their number increased to eighty and afterwards still higher.

The Third Estate or the Commons refused to recognise this right of the clergy and nobility and declared themselves to be the 'Representatives of the Nation', denying the others any right whatsoever in any other capacity than the national representative sitting along with them in the same chamber. Hence, the States General became the 'National Assembly'. They sent invitations to other chamber. Majority of clergy came over to them; 45 of the aristocracy also joined them; then their number increased to eighty and afterwards still higher.

Tennis court oath

The malcontents of nobility and clergy wanted to overthrow the National Assembly. The conspired with ministry. The door of the chamber was shut in the face of the Representatives of the Nation and were guarded by militia. They then proceeded to a tennis court in a body and took an oath never to seperate until they had established a constitution.

Bastille:—

The next day the chamber was again thrown open to them. But secretly thirty thousand troops were mobilised to besiege Paris. The unarmed Parisian Mob attacked Bastille; and Bastille was taken. 14th July 1789

Versailles:—

5th Oct 1789 thousands of men and women proceeded towards Versailles to demand satisfaction from "Garde du Corps" for their insolent behaviour in connection with national cockade. It is known as Versailles expedition. As a result of further developments the king was brought to Paris.

TENNIS COURT OATH

The malcontents of nobility and clergy wanted to overthrow the National Assembly. They conspired with ministry. The door of the chamber was shut in the face of the Representatives of the Nation and were guarded by militia. They then proceeded to a tennis court in a body, and took an oath never to separate until they had established a constitution.

BASTILLE

The next day, the chamber was again thrown open to them. But secretly thirty thousand troops were mobilised to beseige Paris. The unarmed Parisian Mob attacked Bastille; and Bastille was taken.

14th July, 1789

VERSAILLES

5th October, 1789

Thousands of men and women proceeded towards Versailles to demand satisfaction from 'Garde du Corps' for their insolent behaviour in connection with national cockade. It is known as Versailles expedition. As a result of further developments, the King was brought to Paris.

188

The wisdom of every country when properly exerted, is sufficient for all its purposes. (PP. 112 / Re Quan)

: o.

"That the form of a government was a matter wholly at the will of a nation at all times, that if it chose a monarchical form, it had a right to have it so; and if it afterwards chose to be a Republican, it had a right to be a republic: and to say to the King, 'We have no longer any occasion for you.'"

House of Lords. Minister Earl of Shelburne.

o ..

The wisdom of every country when properly exerted, is sufficient for all its purposes.

Rs of Man

: * :

That the form of a government was a matter wholly at the will of a nation all times, if it chose a monarchical form it had a right to have it so; and if it afterwards chose to be a Republican, it had a right to be a republic; and to say to a king, "We have no longer any occasion for you."

House of Lords, Minister Earl of Shelburne

: * :

King: — If there existed a man so transcendently wise above all others, that his wisdom was necessary to instruct a nation, some reason might be offered for monarchy; but when we cast our eyes about a country and observe how every part understands its own affairs; and when we look around the world and see that of all men in it, the race of kings are the most insignificant in capacity, our reason fails to ask us — What are these men kept for? 112.

— : o : —

Libeller: — "If to expose the fraud and imposition of monarchy and every species of hereditary government to lessen the oppression of taxes — to propose plans for the education of helpless infancy, and the comfortable support of the aged and distressed — to endeavour to conciliate nations to each other — to extirpate the horrid practice of war — to promote universal peace, civilization and commerce — and to break the chains of political superstition and raise degraded man to his proper rank — if these things be libellous, let me live the life of a libeller, and let the name of "Libeller" be engraven on my tomb."

— : o : — xi

KING

If there existed a man so transcendently wise above all others, that his wisdom was necessary to instruct a nation, some reason might be offered for monarchy; but when we cast our eyes about a country and observe how every part understands its own affairs; and when we look around the world and see that of all men in it, the race of kings is the most insignificant in capacity, our reason fails to ask us— what are these men kept for?

———————— : * : ————————

LIBELLER

"If to expose the fraud and imposition of monarchy and every species of hereditary government to lessen the oppression of taxes — to propose plans for the education of helpless infancy, and the comfortable support of the aged to distressed — to endeavour to conciliate nations to each other — to extirpate the horrid practice of war — to promote universal peace, civilisation and commerce — and to break the chains of political superstition, and raise degraded man to his proper rank — if these be libellous, let me live the life of libeller, and let the name of 'Libeller' be engraven on my tomb."

———————— : * : ————————

190

But when principle and not place, is the energetic cause of action, a man, I find, is everywhere the same.

: o :

Death: — If we were immortal we should all be miserable; no doubt it is hard to die, but it is sweet to think that we shall not live for ever. [PP. 45. Emile]

: o :

Socialistic Order — "From each according to his ability, to each according to his need."

: o :

Audacity is the ~~soul~~ soul of Success in Revolution.

"Action, Action. Power first discussion afterwards;" said Danton!

: o :

But when principle and not place is the energetic cause of action, a man, I find, is everywhere the same.

———————— : * : ————————

DEATH

If we were immortal we should all be miserable; no doubt it is hard to die, but it is sweet to think that we shall not live for ever.

———————— : * : ————————

SOCIALISTIC ORDER

"From each according to his ability, to each according to his need."

———————— : * : ————————

Audacity is the soul of success in Revolution.

———————— : * : ————————

"Action, Action. Power first, discussion afterwards," said Danton.

———————— : * : ————————

Russian Experiment.
1917-27

"The philosophy of the Bolshevists is utterly, aggressively materialistic, whose one redeeming feature even their bitterest enemies will have to recognize viz. the utter absence of any illusion.

They hold firmly to the faith of their founder that 'Everything can be explained by natural laws or in a narrower sense, by Physiology!'" P30

Philosophers, said Marx, 'have merely interpreted the world in many ways; the really important thing is to change it.'

1. Face and mind of Bolshevism. by Rene Fulop-Miller
2. Russia by [illegible] Mikeen-O'Hara
3. Russian Revolution by Lancelot Lawton (Macmillan)
4. Bolshevist Russia by Anton Karlgren.
5. Literature and Revolution (Trotsky)
6. Marx-Lenin & Science of Revo: by Anton Karlgren

RUSSIAN EXPERIMENT

1917-27

1. Face and Mind of Bolshevism
by Rene Fulop-miller
2. Russia
by Makeev-O' Hara
3. Russian Revolution
by Lancelot Lowton
(Macmillan)
4. Bolshevisk Russia
by Anton Karlgreen
5. Literature and Revolution
Trotsky
6. Marx-Lenin and
Science of Revolution
by Anton Karlgreen

"The philosophy of the Bolsheviks is utterly, aggressively materialistic, whose one redeeming feature even their bitterest enemies will have to recognise, viz. the utter absence of any illusion."

They held firmly to the faith of their founder that "everything can be explained by natural laws or, in a narrower sense, by Physiology!"

"Philosophers," said Marx, "have merely interpreted the world in many ways; the really important thing is to change it."

192 Religion and Socialism:—
"Religion is an opium for mankind" said Marx.

"All idealistic considerations lead in the end to a kind of conception of Divinity, and are, therefore pure non-sense in the eyes of Marxists. Even Hegel saw in God the concrete form of everything good and reasonable that rules the world; the idealist theory must put everything on the shoulders of this unfortunate gray beard, who, according to the teachings of his worshippers, is perfect, and who in addition to Adam, created fleas and harlots, murderers and lepers, hunger and misery, plague and vodka, in order to punish the sinners whom he himself had created, and who sin in accordance with his will.... From the scientific standpoint this theory leads to absurdity. The only scientific explanation of all the phenomenon of the world is supplied by absolute materialism. [(P. 32.) Bukharin]

According to them,

In the beginning Nature; from it life; and from life, thought and all the manifestation we call mental or moral phenomena. There is no such thing as Soull, and Mind is nothing but a function of matter, organized in a particular way. .33.

RELIGION AND SOCIALISM

"Religion is an opium for mankind," said Marx.

All idealistic considerations lead in the end to a kind of conception of Divinity, and are, therefore, pure non-sense in the eyes of Marxists. Even Hegal saw in God the concrete form of everything good and reasonable that rules the world; the idealist theory must put everything on the shoulders of this unfortunate grey beard, who, according to the teachings of his worshippers, is perfect, and who, in addition to Adam, created fleas and harlots, murderers and lepers, hunger and misery, plague and vodka, in order to punish the sinners whom he himself had created, and who sin in accordance with his will. . . . From the scientific standpoint, ths theory leads to absurdity. The only scientific explanation of all the phenomena of the world is supplied by absolute materialism.

According to them, in the beginning, Nature; from it life; and from life, thought and all the manifestations we call mental or moral phenomenon. There is no such thing as Soul, and Mind is nothing but a function of matter, organised in a particular way.

Marx on Insurrection:—

Firstly. "never play with insurrection if there is no determination to drive it to the bitter end (literally— to face all the consequences of this play). An insurrection is an equation with very indefinite magnitudes, the value of which may change every day. The forces to be opposed have all the advantages of organization, discipline and traditional authority.
If the rebels cannot bring great forces to bear against their antagonists, they will be smashed and destroyed.

Secondly:— The insurrection once started, it is necessary to act with the utmost determination and pass over to the offensive. The defensive is the death of every armed rising; it perishes before it has measured forces with the enemy. The antagonists must be surprised while their soldiers are still scattered, and new successes, however small, must be attained daily; the moral ascendancy given by the first success, must be kept up. One must rally to the side of insurrection the vacillating elements, which always follow the stronger, and which always look out for the safer side. .. In one word, act according to the words of Danton — the greatest master of Revolutionary policy yet known.— 'Audacity — audacity and yet again audacity.'

MARX ON INSURRECTION

Firstly, never play with insurrection if there is no determination to drive it to the bitter end (literally — to face all the consequences of this play). An insurrection is an equation with very indefinite magnitudes, the value of which may change every day. The forces to be opposed have all the advantages of organisation, discipline and traditional authority.

If the rebels cannot bring great forces to bear against their antagonists, they will be smashed and destroyed.

Secondly, the insurrection once started, it is necessary to act with the utmost determination and pass over the offensive. The defensive is the death of every armed rising; it perishes before it has measured forces with the enemy. The antagonists must be surprised while their soldiers are still scattered, and new successes, however small, must be attained daily; the moral ascendancy given by the first success, must be kept up. One must rally to the side of insurrection the vacillating elements, which always follow the stronger, and which always look out for the safer side. . . . In one word, act according to the words of Danton — the greatest master of Revolutionary policy yet known — Audacity — audacity — and yet again audacity!

---

* Page 194 to 272 are blank.

... Do you want an expansion of the Legislative councils? Do you want that a few Indians shall sit as your representatives in the House of Commons? Do you want a large number of Indians in the Civil Service? Let us see whether 50, 100, 200 or 300 civilians will make the Govt. our own.... The whole civil service might be Indian, but the civil servants have to carry out orders — they can not direct, they can not dictate the policy. One swallow does not make the summer. One civilian, 100, or 1000 civilians in the service of the British Govt. will not make the Govt. Indian. There are traditions, they are laws, there are policies to which every civilian, be he black or brown or white, must submit, and as long as these traditions have not been altered, as long as these principles have not been amended, as long as that policy has not been radically changed, the supplanting of Europeans by Indian agency will not make for self government in this country....

If the Govt. were to come and tell me today, "Take Swaraj," I would say thank you for the gift but I will not have that which I can not acquire by my own hand..........

.... we shall in the imperative compel the submission to our will of any power that may set itself against us.

... the Primary thing is the prestige of the Govt.

...Do you want an expansion of the Legislative Councils? Do you want that a few Indians shall sit as your representatives in the House of Commons? Do you want a large number of Indians in the Civil Service? Let us see whether 50, 100, 200 or 300 civilians will make the Government our own...The whole Civil Service might be Indian, but the civil servants have to carry out orders — they cannot direct, they cannot dictate the policy. One swallow does not make the summer. One civilian, 100 or 1000 civilians in the service of the British Government will not make the Government Indian. There are traditions, there are laws, there are policies to which every civilian, be he black or brown or white, must submit; and as long as these traditions have not been altered, as long as these principles have not been amended, as long as that policy has not been radically changed, the supplanting of Europeans by Indian agency will not make for self-government in this country . . .

If the Government were to come and tell me today, "Take swaraj," I would say thank you for the gift, but I will not have that which I cannot acquire by my own hand . . .

We shall in the imperative compel the submission to our will of any power that may set itself against us.

....The Primary thing is the prestige of the Government.

274

Is really self government within the Empire a practicable ideal? What would it mean? It would mean either no real self-government for us or no real over lordship for England. Would we be satisfied with the shadow of self-government? If not, would England be satisfied with the shadow of over lordship? In either case England would not be satisfied with a shadowy overlordship, and we refuse to be satisfied with a shadowy self-government. And therefore no ~~self government~~ compromise is possible under such conditions between self-govt. in India and the overlordship of England. If self-govt. — (real) is conceded to us, what would be England's position not only in India, but in British Empire itself? Self--govt. means the right of self-taxation; it means the right of self-control, it means the right of the people to impose protective and prohibitive tariffs on foreign imports. The moment we have the right of selftaxation, what shall we do? We shall not try to be engaged in this uphill work of industrial boycott. But we shall do what every nation has done. Under the circumstances in which we live now, we shall impose a heavy prohibitive protective tariff upon every inch of textile fabric from Manchester, upon every blade of knife that comes from Leeds. We shall refuse to grant admittance to a British soul into our territory. We would not allow British capital to be engaged in the development of Indian resources, as it is now engaged. We would not ~~allow~~ grant any right to the British capitalists to dig up

Is really self-government within the Empire a practicable idea? What would it mean? It would mean either no real self-government for us or no real over-lordship for England. Would we be satisfied with the shadow of self-government? If not, would England be satisfied with the shadow of overlordship? In either case, England would not be satisfied with a shadowy overlordship, and we refuse to be satisfied with a shadowy self-government. And, therefore, no compromise is possible under such conditions between self-government in India and the overlordship of England . . . If self-government (real) is conceded to us, what would be England's position not only in India, but in British Empire itself? Self-government means the right of self-taxation; it means the right of self-control; it means the right of the people to impose protective and prohibitive tariffs on foreign imports. The moment we have the right of self-taxation, what shall we do? We shall not try to be engaged in this uphill work of industrial boycott. But we shall do what every nation has done. Under the circumstances in which we live now, we shall impose a heavy, prohibitive, protective tariff upon every inch of textile fabric from Manchester, upon every blade of knife that comes from Leeds. We shall refuse to grant admittance to a British soul into our territory. We would not allow British capital to be engaged in the development of Indian resources, as it is now engaged. We would not grant any right to the British capitalists to dig.

(contd.)

the mineral wealth of the land and to carry it to their own isles. We shall want foreign capital. But we shall apply for foreign loans in the open markets of the whole world, guaranteeing the credit of the Indian Govt., the Indian nation, for the repayment of the loan...... And England's commercial interests would not be furthered in the way these are being furthered now, under the condition of popular self-government, though it might be within the Empire. But what would it mean within the Empire? It would mean that England would have to enter into some arrangements with us for some preferential tariff. England would have to come to our markets on the conditions that we would impose upon her for the purpose, if she wanted an open door in India, and after a while, when we have developed our resources a little and organized our industrial life, we would want the open door not only to England, but to every part of the British Empire. And do you think it is possible for a small country like England with a handful of population, although she might be enormously wealthy, to compete on fair and equitable terms with a mighty continent like India with immense natural resources, with her teeming populations, the soberest and most abstemious populations known to any part of the world?

If we have really self-government within the Empire, if we 300 millions of people have that freedom of the Empire, the Empire would cease to be British. It would be the Indian Empire, ...

Ref. B. C. Pal. New Spirit 1907.

up the mineral wealth of the land and to carry it to their own isles. We shall want foreign capital. But we shall apply for foreign loans in the open markets of the whole world, guaranteeing the credit of the Indian Government, the Indian Nation, for the repayment of the loan . . . And England's commercial interests would not be furthered in the way these are being furthered now, under the condition of popular self-government, though it might be within the Empire. But what whould it mean within the Empire? It would mean that England would have to enter into some arrangements with us for some preferential tariff. England would have to come to our markets on the conditions that we would impose upon her for the purpose, if she wanted an open door in Indian, and after a while, when we have developed our resources a little and organised our industrial life, we would want the open door not only to England, but to every part of British Empire. And do you think it is possible for a small country like England with a handful of population, although she might be enormously wealthy, to compete on fair and equitable terms with a mighty continent like India with immense natural resources, with her teeming population, the soberest and most abstemious population known to any part of the world?

If we have really self-government within the Empire, if 300 millions of people have that freedom of the Empire, the Empire would cease to be British. It would be the Indian Empire...

Bip. Ch. Pal

New Spirit, 1907

276

Hindu Civilization:—

It may seem to us to present in many of its aspects an almost unthinkable combination of spiritualistic idealism and of gross materialism, of asceticism and of sensuousness, of over weening arrogance when it identifies the human self with the universal self and merges man in the Divinity and the Divinity in man, and of demoralising pessimism when it preaches that life itself is but a painful allusion and that the sovereign remedy and end of all evils is non-existence.

Chirol. 26 P.
Indian unrest.

— .·. —

Educational Policy:—

The main original object of the introduction of Western Education into India was the training of a sufficient number of young Indians to fill the subordinate posts in the public offices with English-speaking natives. P. 34

— .·. —

HINDU CIVILISATION

It may seem to us to present in many of its aspects in almost unthinkable combination of spiritualistic idealism and of gross materialism, of asceticism and of sensuousness, of overweening arrogance when it identifies the human self with the universal self and merges man in the Divinity and the Divinity in man, and of demoralising pessimism when it preaches that life itself is but a painful allusion and that the sovereign remedy and end of all evils is non-existence.

Indian Unrest

———————: * :———————

EDUCATION POLICY

The main original object of the introduction of Western Education into Indian was the training of a sufficient number of young Indians to fill the subordinate posts in the public offices with English-speaking natives.

How many of the western educated Indians who have thrown themselves into political agitation against the tyranny of the British bureaucracy have ever raised a finger to free their own fellow-country-men from the tyranny of those social evils? How many of them are entirely free from it themselves, or, if free, have the courage to act up to their opinion?

India Old and New P. 107

Jail Diary-277

How many of the Western educated Indians who have thrown themselves into political agitation against the tyranny of the British bureaucracy have ever raised a finger to free their own fellow countrymen from the tyranny of those social evils? How many of them are entirely free from it themselves or, if free, have the courage to act up to their opinion?

India Old & New

278

No Indian Parliament Conceivable)

The Indian National Congress assumed unto itself almost from the beginning the function of a Parliament. There was and is no room for a Parliament in India, because, so long as British rule remained a reality, the Govt of India, as Lord Morley has plainly stated, must be an autocracy—benevolent and full of sympathy with Indian ideas, but still an autocracy. 154. Unrest.

Aim or goal of the Congress

'The Objects of the Indian National Congress are the attainment by the people of India of a system of Govt. similar to that enjoyed by the self-governing members of the British Empire and a participation by them in the rights and responsibilities of the Empire on equal terms."

Malviyaji from the Chair in 1909 Lahore Session of the Congress

---

NO INDIAN PARLIAMENT CONCEIVABLE!

The Indian National Congress assumed into itself, almost from the beginning, the function of a Parliament. There was and is no room for a Parliament in India, because, so long as British rule remains a reality, the Government of India, as Lord Morley has plainly stated, must be an auto- cracy — benevolent and full of sympathy with Indian ideas, but still an autocracy.

: * :

AIM OR GOAL OF THE CONGRESS

The objects of the Indian National Congress are the attainment by the people of India of a system of Government similar to that enjoyed by the self-government members of the British Empire and a participation by them in the rights and responsibilities of the Empire on equal terms.

Malviyaji from the Chair

in 1907 Lahore Session of the Congress

: * :

Re: Constitution of Free India

No one but the voice of the Mother herself will can determine when once She comes to herself and stands free what constitution shall be adopted by her for the guidance of her life after the revolution is over.... Without going into detail we may mention this much, that whether the head of the Imperial Govt of the Indian nation be a President or a King depends upon how the revolution develops itself.... The Mother must be free, must be one and united, must make her will supreme. Then it may be that She gives out this her will either wearing a kingly crown on her head or a Republican mantle round her sacred form.

Forget not, O Princes! that a strict account will be asked of your doings and non-doings, and a people newly-born will not fail to pay in the coin you paid. Every one who shall have actively betrayed the trust of the people, disowned his fathers, and debased his blood by arraying himself against the Mother — he shall be crushed to dust and ashes... Do you doubt our grim earnestness? If so hear the name of Dhingra and be dumb. In the name of that martyr, O Indian princes, we ask you to think solemnly and deeply upon these words. Choose as you will and you will reap what you sow. Choose whether you shall be the first of the nation's fathers or the last of nation's tyrants.

P. 14 Indian unrest
"Choose O Princes"

Untouchability: —

From the political point of view the conversion of so many millions of the population of India to the faith of their rulers would open the prospects of such moment that I need not expatiate upon them. P. 184

RE : CONSTITUTION OF FREE INDIA

No one but the voice of the Mother herself will and can determine when once she comes to herself and stands free, what constitution shall be adopted by Her for the guidance of Her life after the revolution is over. . . . Without going into detail we may mention this much, that whether the head of the Imperial Government of the Indian nation be a President or a King depends upon how the revolution develops itself. . . . The mother must be free, must be one and united, must make Her will supreme. Then it may be that she gives out this Her will either wearing a kingly crown on her head or a Republican mantle round her sacred form.

Forget not, O Princes! that a strict account will be asked of your doings and non-doings, and a people newly born will not fail to pay in the coin you paid. Everyone who shall have actively betrayed the trust of the people, disowned his fathers, and debased his blood by arraying himself against the Mother — he shall be crushed to dust and ashes . . . Do you doubt our earnestness? If so, hear the name of Dhingra and be dumb. In the name of that martyr, O Indian princes, we ask you to think solemnly and deeply upon these words. Choose as you will and you will reap what you sow. Choose whether you shall be the first of the nation's fathers or the last of nation's tyrants.

Indian Unrest

Choose O' Princes

———————— : * : ————————

UNTOUCHABLES

From the political point of view the conversion of so many millions of the populations of India to the faith of their rulers would open the prospects of such moments that I need not expatiate upon them.

280

[illegible] Hatya guru Yagna

Tempted by gold some native devils in form of men
the disgrace of India — the police — arrested those great
men Birendra Ghosh and others who worked for the
freedom of their country by sacrificing their
interests and dedicating their lives in the performance
of the sacred ceremony of "Jagna" (?) preparing
bombs. The greatest of these devils in human
form Ashutosh Bishwas began to pave for these
heroes the way to the gallows. Bravo Charu!
(the murderer of Biswas) all honour to your
parents to glorify them, to show the highest
degree of courage disregarding the paltry
short span of life you removed the figure of
that monster from the world. Not long ago
the whites by force and trick plundered in
from the Indians. That mean wretch
Shams-ul-alam who espoused the
cause of the enemies of Alamgir Badshah
who put a stain on the name of his forefathers
for the sake of gold — today you have removed
that fiend from the sacred soil of India.
From Naren Gosain to Lalit Chakravarti
all turned approvers through the ~~[illegible]~~
machination of that fiendish wizard

HATYA NOT YAGNA

Tempted by gold, some native devils in form of men, the disgrace of India — the police — arrested those great men Barindra Ghose and others who worked for the freedom of their country by sacrificing their interests and dedicating their lives in the performance of the sacred ceremony of 'Yagna', preparing bombs. The greatest of these devils in human form, Ashutosh Biswas began to pave for these heroes the way to the gallows. Bravo Charu! (the murderer of Biswas) all honour to your parents to glorify them, to show the highest degree of courage, disregarding the paltry short span of life, you removed the figure of that monster from the world. Not long ago, the Whites, by force and trick, filched India from the Indians. That mean wretch Shamas-ul-Alam, who espoused the cause of gold ... today you have removed that fiend from the sacred soil of India. From Naren Gosain to Talit Chakravarti, all turned approvers through the machinations of that fiendish wizard.

Shams-ul-alam and by his torture had you not removed that ally of the monsters could there be any hope for India.

Many have raised the cry that to rebel is a great sin but what is rebellion. Is there anything in India to rebel against? Can a Feringhi be recognized as the king of India whose very touch whose mere shadow compells Hindus to purify themselves.

These are merely western robbers looting India.... Extirpate them ye good sons of India! wherever you find them without mercy, and with them their spies and their secret agents. Last year and their secret agents. nineteen lakhs of men died of fever, small pox, cholera, plague and other diseases in Bengal alone. While yourselves fortunate that you were not counted amongst those but remember that plague and cholera may attack you tomorrow, and is it not better for you to die like heroes?

When God was so ordained, think ye not that at this auspicious moment it is the duty of every good son of India to slay these white enemies? Do not allow yourself

Shamas-ul-Alam and by his torture had you not removed that ally of monsters, could there be any hope for India.

Many have raised the cry that to rebel is a great sin, but what is rebellion? Is there anything in India to rebel against? Can a Feringhi be recognised as the King of India whose very touch, whose mere shadow compels Hindus to purify themselves?

These are merely Western robbers looting India. . . . Extirpate them, ye good sons of India! wherever you find them, without mercy, and with them their spies and secret agents. Last year, 19 lakh men died of fever, small pox, cholera, plague and other diseases in Bengal alone. Think yourself fortunate that you were not counted amongst those, but remember that plague and cholera may attack you tomorrow, and is it not better for you to die as heroes?

When God has so ordained, think ye not that at this auspicious moment, it is the duty of every good son of India to slay these white enemies? Do not allow yourselves.

282

to die of plague and cholera thus polluting the sacred soil of the Mother India. Our Shastras are our guide for discriminating between virtue and vice. Our Shastras repeatedly tell us that the killing of these white fiends and of their aiders and abettors is equal to a great ceremonial sacrifice (ashwamedh yagna). Come one and all, let us offer our sacrifice before the altar in chorus and pray that in this ceremony all white elephants may perish in the flames as the vipers perished in the serpents slaying ceremony of Janma Yagna. Keep in mind that "it is not murder but yagna; a sacrificial rite."

{P 342. notes}

I. U.

"Total electors in India 62,00,000 viz $2\frac{3}{4}\%$ of the total population throughout India and in direct British administration, excluding the areas to which the 1919 act was not to be applied."

194 I.O.N.

to die of plague and cholera, thus polluting the sacred soil of the Mother India. Our Shastras are our guide for discriminating between virtue and vice. Our Shastras repeatedly tell us that the killing of these white fiends and of their aiders and abettors is equal to a great ceremonial sacrifice (Aswamedh yagna). Come, one and all, let us offer our sacrifice before the altar in chrous, and pray that in this ceremony all white serpents may perish in its flames as the vipers perished in the serpent-slaying ceremony of Janma (jay) Yagna. Keep in mind that it is not murder but yagna; a sacrificial rite.

I.U.

"Total electors in India are 62,00,000, viz. 2¾% of the total population throughout India under direct British administration, excluding the areas to which the 1919 Act was not to be applied."

I.O.N.

India Old & New : Chirol 6.

'The British people will have to beware that if they do not want to do justice, it will be the bounden duty of every Indian to destroy the Empire.' Mahatmaji (Nagpur Congress)

191

Rural & Urban Question :—

Some official ingenuity had been displayed in grouping small towns together without any regard for geography, in order to prevent townsmen undesirably addicted to advanced political views from standing as candidates for the rural constituencies in which many of the smaller towns would otherwise have been naturally merged. This was a last effort based on the old belief that the population of the Punjab could be divided into goats and sheep, the goats being the 'disloyal' townsmen and the sheep being the 'loyal' peasantry.

Was also Chief of Times in 1932

INDIA – OLD AND NEW : CHIROL, V.

"The British people will have to beware that if they do not want to do justice, it will be the bounden duty of every Indian to destory the Empire."

Mahatmaji (Nagpur Congress)

: * :

RURAL AND URBAN QUESTIONS

Some official ingenuity had been displayed in grouping remote towns together without any regard for geography, in order to prevent townsmen undesirably addicted to advanced political view from standing as candidates for the rural constituencies in which many of the smaller towns would otherwise have been naturally merged. This was the last effort based on the old belief that the population of the Punjab could be divided into goats and sheep, the goats being the 'disloyal' townsmen and the sheep being the 'loyal' peasantry.

: * :

Khalsa College was opened in 1802.

284

India as I knew it !

Truly the path of a 'Mahatma' is difficult, and it is not surprising that Gandhi was recently tried to repudiate the title — and its responsibilities. His influence in India is steadily waning, but his ascetic pose and the vague impracticable Tolstoyan theories which he so skilfully enunciates as great moral truths, seem to have deluded many well meaning but weak minded people in sentimental England and some even in logical France who are on the lookout for a new light from the east." — P. 65

Informer.—

The failure of the authorities in that case to conceal and protect the informer (or approver James Carey who betrayed the Invincible gang of the revolutionaries and due to whose evidence Brady, Fitzharris and Mullet were hanged for the Phoenix Park double murder i.e. of chief and under Secretaries. The informer was shot dead on board at Durban by a young revolutionary O'Donnell) even though his assassin was brought to justice, was I believe, one of the chief reasons why the supply of that contemptible but useful class, previously so common in Irish Conspiracies, ran dry at the source. As Lieut. Governor of Punjab, before and during the Great War, I had to deal with many revolutionary conspiracies, in unravelling which the [illegible] informer played a considerable role, and our precautions were so thorough that not in a single case did an informer come to any injury.

INDIA AS I KNEW IT!

"Truly the path of a 'Mahatma' is difficult, and it is not surprising that Gandhi has recently tried to repudiate the title — and its responsibilities. His influence in India is steadily waning, but his asectic pose and the vague impracticable Tolstoyan theories which he so skilfully enunciates as great moral truths, seem to have deluded many well-meaning but weak-minded people in sentimental England and some even in logical France, who are on the look out for a new light from the East."

INFORMER

The failure of the authorities in that case to conceal and protect the informer (or James Carey who betrayed the Invincible gang of the revolutionaries and due to whose, evidence Brady. Fitzherbert and Mullen were hanged for the Phoenix Park double murder, i.e. of Chief and Under-Secretaries. The informer was shot dead on board at Durban by a young revolutionary, O'Donnell) even though his assassin was brought to justice, was, I believe, one of chief reasons why the supply of that contemptible, but useful class, previously so common in Irish Conspiracies, ran dry at the source. As Lieutenant Governor of Punjab, before and during the Great War, I had to deal with many revolutionary conspiracies, in unravelling which the genius informer played a considerable role, and our precautions were so thorough that not in a single case did an informer come to any injury.

(cintd.)

———— : * : ————

One can imagine how thoroughly the Indian conspirator, with his low cunning, abnormal vanity, inborn aptitude for intrigue, and capacity for glossing over unpleasant facts, was at home in this atmosphere

P. 187
India as I knew it

Arya Samaj

In fact the Arya Samaj is a nationalist revival against Western influence; it urges its followers in the Satyarth Prakash, the authoritative work of Dayanand, who was the founder of the sect, to go back to the Vedas, and to seek the golden future in the imaginary golden past of the Aryas. The Satyarth Prakash also contains arguments against non-Hindu rule, and a leading organ of the sect a few years ago claimed Dayanand as the real author of the doctrine of Swaraj.

However, the Arya Samaj in 1907 thought it wise to publish a resolution to the effect that as mischievous people were and are spread rumors hostile to them, the organization in reiterating its old creed declared that it had no connection of any kind with any political body or with any political agitation in any shape. While accepting this declaration as disassociating the samaj ~~as a body~~ from extremist politics, it should be noted in fairness to the orthodox Hindus that while the Samaj does not include perhaps ~~more than~~ 5% of the Hindu population of the Punjab, an enormous ~~[illegible]~~ proportion of the Hindus convicted of sedition and other political offences from 1907 down to the present day are members of the Samaj.

P. 186 2nd

Jail Diary-285

One can imagine how thoroughly the Indian conspirator, with his low cunning, normal vanity, inborn aptitude for intrigue, and capacity for glossing over unpleasant facts, was at home in this atmosphere.

India as I Knew It

: * :

Arya Samaj

In fact, the Arya Samaj is a nationalist revival against Western influence; it urges its followers in the *Satyarth Prakash*, the authoritative work of Dayanand, who was the founder of the sect, to go back to the Vedas, and to seek the golden future in the imaginary golden past of the Aryas. The *Satyarath Prakash* also contains arguments against non-Hindu rule, and a leading organ of the sect, few years ago, claimed Dayanand as the real author of the doctrine of Swaraj.

However, the Arya Samaj in 1907, thought it wise to publish a resolution to the effect that as mischievous people here and there spread rumours hostile to them, the organisation in reiterating its old creed, declared that it had no connection of any kind with any political body or with any political agitation in any shape. While accepting this declaration as disassociating the Samaj as a body from extremist politics, it should be noted in fairness to the orthodox Hindus that while the Samaj does not include perhaps more than 5% of the Hindu population of the Punjab, an enormous proportion of the Hindus convicted of sedition and other political offences from 1907 down to the present day, are members of the Samaj.

: * :

286

Statistical figures about India :—

In England & Wales $\frac{4}{5}$ of people live in towns.

Standard of urban life begins when 1000 people live together. Only then Municipal drainage, lighting & water supply can be organized.

India (British)
Out of total 244000,000, 226000000 live in villages.

England in normal times give to Industry 58% of people to Industry
8% to agriculture

India gives 71% to agriculture
12% to Industry
5% to trade
2% to domestic service
$1\frac{1}{2}$% to independent Professions
$1\frac{1}{2}$% to Govt service including Army.

In whole of India 226 millions out of 315 millions are supported by soil
208 millions out of them live or depend directly upon the agriculture.

(Montford Report)

STATISTICAL FIGURES ABOUT INDIA

In England and Wales 4/5 of people live in towns. Standard of urban life begins when 1000 people live together. Only then Municipal drainage, lighting and water supply can be organised.	India (British) out of total 244000,000 226000,000 live in villages.

England–in normal times gives
58% of people to Industry
8% to Agriculture.
India gives: 71% to Agriculture
12% to Industry
5% to Trade
2% to Domestic Service
1½% to independent Professions
1½% to Government Service, including Army.

In whole of India, 226 millions out of 315 millions are supported by soil. 208 millions out of them live or depend directly upon agriculture.

Montford Report

Total Area 1,800,000 square miles
20 times of Great Britain
700,000 sq miles or more than $\frac{1}{3}$ are under
States' control. Indian States are 600 in number.
Burma is greater than France.
Madras & Bombay are greater than Italy
seperately.

Total population of India (1921 Census)
318,942,000
i.e. $\frac{1}{5}$ th of the whole human race.
247,000,000 are in British
India and 71,900,000 in States.

$2\frac{1}{2}$ million persons were literate in
English. 16 in every thousand males and 2
in every thousand female.

Total Number of vernaculars is 222
Total number of villages 500,000

Total area –1,800,000 square miles
20 times of Great Britain

700,000 square miles, or more than ⅓ are under States' control. Indian States are 600 in number. Burma is greater than France. Madras and Bombay are greater than Italy separately.

Total population of India (1921 census) – 318,942,000
i.e. ⅕ of the whole human race.

247,000,000 are in British India and 71,900,000 in States.

2½ million persons were literate in English — 16 in every thousand males and 2 in every thousand females.

Total Number of vernaculars is 222
Total Number of villages is 500,000

Suez Canal opened in 1869.

Total Export of India at that time was
Rs. 80 crores = £ 80,000,000.

1926-27 and preceding two years the average
was Rs. 350 crores i.e. about £ 262,500,000.

Total population 319 millions out of which
32 $\frac{1}{2}$ millions i.e. 10.2% live in towns &
Cities (urban) while in England the
percentage is 79%

And the most difficult part of the
task will be to instil into the
minds of the slum dwellers
themselves the desire for
something better.

Pp. 22

Simon Report.

□□□